Lewisias

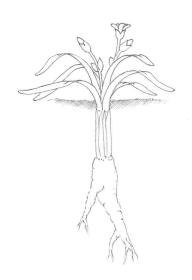

Meriwether Lewis, 1774–1809

LEWISIAS

by

B. LeRoy Davidson

Foreword by Sean Hogan
Illustrations by Micheal Moshier

TIMBER PRESS
Portland, Oregon

Frontispiece: Meriwether Lewis by Charles Willson Peale, c. 1807, oil on wood panel; reproduced with the kind permission of the Independence National Historical Park Collection.

Endpapers: "A map of Lewis and Clark's track, across the western portion of North America," 1814, Library of Congress, Geography and Map Division, Washington, D.C.

Published in 2000 by
TIMBER PRESS, Inc.
The Haseltine Building
133 S.W. Second Avenue, Suite 450
Portland, Oregon 97204, U.S.A.

Printed in Hong Kong • Designed by Susan Applegate

Library of Congress Cataloging-in-Publication Data
Davidson, B. LeRoy.
Lewisias/by B. LeRoy Davidson; with illustrations by Micheal Moshier.
    p.   cm.
Includes bibliographical references (p.   ).
ISBN 0-88192-447-4
1. Lewisia. I. Title.
SB413.L48 D38 2000
635.9'3353—dc21   99-053481

Contents

Foreword Ho!

L EWISIAS have been popular garden subjects since the mid nineteenth century. Their bright flowers and tidy succulent nature captivate most who see them, and it could be hazarded that hardly an alpine or rock garden exists without one or several. With only a few specific requirements, many of the taxa and their cultivars and hybrids settle very nicely into the rock garden, trough, or coolhouse. Exciting to both the horticulturist and the botanist are the several new species and varieties that have emerged only in the last few years. They frequently inhabit remote, inaccessible, and often very specific areas of rugged western North America; it is certainly possible that more are yet to be discovered.

Roy Elliott's 1966 monograph *The Genus Lewisia*, published by the Alpine Garden Society, clarified several points but also pointed out several holes in our understanding of the genus and its habitats. Brian Mathew's 1989 Kew Magazine monograph updated much information and certainly made even more clarifications, in a somewhat less anecdotal yet informative fashion. Roy Davidson, with much the same cast of characters, looks at the plants not only from a horticultural and studied taxonomic view but from a naturalist's perspective. Having spent many a day scrambling across a scree slope with him, or searching for that shale cliff that ought to be there according to the topo map, I can attest that his knowledge is literally hands-on, including a little dirt under the fingernails. Although thoughts on the species' taxonomic status are ever evolving and ever-more sophisticated methods of learning are being used, Roy's perspective seems, refreshingly, almost of the plants themselves.

Roy's contributions to horticulture are numerous, and his influence on Northwest horticulture, in particular, great. In the last forty years his more than sixty-five additions to the literature, many of which first appeared in the *Bulletin* of the North American Rock Garden Society, have ranged from articles on the genera *Penstemon, Iris, Erythronium, Synthyris,* and *Bergenia* to—of course—*Lewisia*. He has also written about the family Diapensiaceae, among others, and of his travels to see plants in habitat—the ultimate learning experience.

The same ability to teach and observe has led to his many horticultural selections, both in his abundant garden and in the wild: the well-known *Pulmonaria* 'Roy Davidson', *Iris* 'Roy Davidson', the recently introduced *Chaenomeles japonica* 'Atsuya Hamata', and *Lewisia rediviva* 'Teanaway Rose', among many others. It is no wonder that Roy's name is spun into so many stories of how certain plants came into our midst.

As the following pages attest, Roy's interests go beyond the botanical and horticultural aspects of the plants to the people who have interacted with them: from Sacajawea, the Shoshone woman who helped guide Lewis and Clark through the American West, to the many other explorers, botanists, and plants people who have "discovered," named (renamed!), and otherwise labored over the genus *Lewisia*, studying its distribution and conditions in the wild, sorting out its often confusing taxonomy, or bringing out the horticultural potential we now enjoy. Not surprisingly these people are concentrated in a couple of regions. Oregon's Rogue River valley and the Pacific West Coast, the heart of lewisia country, is home to many of the early growers—and to the original plants selected for cultivation from the nearby mountains. And certainly enthusiasts in Europe, especially the United Kingdom, have taken lewisias to new heights. Much has been learned about cultivation techniques, and even more people are behind the wonderful new hybrids and color strains that have been developed in recent years.

Roy encapsulates a history and brings an understanding of lewisias through a point of view both personal and insightful. He does so with humor, often tongue-in-cheek, and the ability to tell a story that makes one feel as if they were trudging across that ridgetop right alongside him. I am honored to be a very small part of this book and to have been able to know and work with Roy.

SEAN HOGAN

CHAPTER ONE

A Voyage of Discovery

The genus *Lewisia*, comprising about twenty species at present and restricted in its distribution to western North America, has been an object of lifelong fascination for botanists, wildflower enthusiasts, and rock gardeners the world round. Discovered on the famous Lewis and Clark expedition, the genus holds an incomparably high place in the history of western American exploration, proudly bearing the name of explorer Meriwether Lewis. The tangled taxonomic history of the genus is fairly typical of the tumult that ensued as the science of botany passed slowly from the capable hands of explorers to those of biochemists and statisticians, offering a unique view into two intersecting realms of the human interest in plants—scientific botany and horticulture.

With lewisias, as with most things, it is best to start at the beginning, which for our purposes is the afternoon of 4 May 1804. On this day, a military party of exploration left Saint Louis, Missouri, under the leadership of captains Meriwether Lewis and William Clark. Their mandate from President Thomas Jefferson was to map out a route to the Pacific Coast by following the Missouri River northwest to its source, crossing the Rocky Mountains, and finally descending from the heights of the Rocky Mountain nexus to the mouth of the Columbia River, which territory Boston sea captain Robert Gray had claimed for the United States in 1792.

An important part of Lewis and Clark's task was the collection of natural specimens, including plants. Jefferson instructed Lewis to study "the

soil and face of the country; its growth and vegetable productions especially those not of the United States." Tradition has it in Philadelphia that
the idea for the expedition was hatched in Bernard McMahon's seed store,
a shop on Market Street just below Second which was frequented by naturalists and gardeners. Such a junket had been discussed there for many
years among such cronies as John Bartram and Benjamin Franklin—both
principal founders of Philadelphia's American Philosophical Society—
and later by Bartram's son William and the botanist Benjamin Barton,
among many others. Thomas Jefferson himself paid an occasional visit to
McMahon's, and the German botanist Frederick Pursh was employed
there for some time.

The more than thirty members of the traveling expedition lived off the
land during their eighteen months of travel. They were able to barter with
the women of the Mandan nation of the northern Great Plains for such
familiar cultivated plant foods as corn, beans, squash, and pumpkins.
Their meat was buffalo, elk, deer—"whatever moved." Further on, aided
by their Shoshone guide Sacajawea, the party enjoyed many of the native
vegetables she had indicated. When they wintered on the Pacific Coast,
they exchanged goods for various berries and roots, such as yampah, ca-
mass, and wapato. Such native food plants formed an important part of
the botanical collections as well.

On their outward journey to the Pacific, the party had several en-
counters with spaetlum, a ropy, thong-like root dug and eaten fresh by
American Indians as an emergency food, or dried and carried as a staple
during travel to their buffalo hunting grounds. In high summer, August
1805, on the upper reaches of the Missouri, Lewis had his first taste of
roots that were new to him: brittle, white, and cylindrical, they obviously
had been stored for some time and were about the size of a small quill.
Earlier that day, the expedition's hunter had surprised a small party of
Indians who had stopped to make a meal of dried roots, game being
scarce. They fled, leaving behind a parcel of these desiccated roots, which
were conveyed to Lewis. Lewis heated them until they were softened but

still found them "bitter and naucious to the pallatte, although the natives eat them heartily."

Lewis was not to see the growing plant until his return, when on 1 July 1806 he noted it near their old campsite at Traveller's Rest. His acquisitions notebook records merely that he had "met with a singular plant"; he made no entry in his diary for this day of rest, immediately following the difficult crossing of the Rockies, in deep snow, with little food for man or beast. We can only wonder whether he recognized that the blossom of his singular find had sprung from the root that had so offended his tastebuds the previous season.

This campsite is situated on the Bitterroot River near the village of Lolo in Missoula County, Montana, where Lolo Creek flows eastward from the Rocky Mountains but still to the west of their summit, at approximately 3400 feet (1035 meters) elevation, in a broad, sandy valley amid the granitic mountains now known as the Bitterroot Range. This valley was a favorite site for the inhabitants of the area to gather bitterroot. (Bitterroot, the English common name for spaetlum or *Lewisia rediviva*, is a translation of *racine amère*, the name given the plant by French-speaking trappers.) Lewis found his specimens on stony areas elevated from the valley gravels, growing along with *Sedum stenopetalum*, *Orthocarpus tenuifolius*, *Trifolium* species, and *Oxytropis nana*.

Exactly how German botanist Frederick Traugott Pursh (1774–1820) came to possess and describe Lewis's botanical collections has never been fully explained. We know few details of Pursh's life. Saxon-born and educated in Dresden, he traveled in 1799 to Baltimore, where he found employment as a gardener. By 1802, he had been made caretaker of Woodlands, the estate of William Hamilton, and had become well known in the Philadelphia community of natural philosophers. He counted Thomas Jefferson as a friend.

It is likely that all the botanical acquisitions of Lewis and Clark were originally intended to go to Professor Benjamin Barton at the College of Philadelphia, with whom Lewis had taken a brief crash course in the techniques of botanical collection just before his departure in 1803 and who planned writing a book about the plants. Indeed, Lewis sent Barton botanical specimens from Fort Mandan on the expedition's westbound trip. There are various stories of how the remainder of Lewis and Clark collections were disposed, and not all agree. Pursh declared that the material was put into his hands by Lewis himself, and in fact, Bernard McMahon had written Lewis in Saint Louis to recommend Pursh as "a very intelligent and practical Botanist, who would be well inclined to render you any service in his power." In another version of the story, Pursh was away on a mission for Barton when that portion of the Lewis and Clark collection arrived in Philadelphia, and President Jefferson directed that it be delivered to the seedsman McMahon (whom Pursh later honored in naming the genus *Mahonia*). One way or the other, the material was put temporarily in McMahon's hands in April of 1807.

By the time the cooler days of fall 1807 were advanced, the bitterroot collection, in characteristic fashion, had begun to put out its little green points of foliage. Noting this, McMahon, according to Pursh, "coaxed it into growth and exhibited it in his store," where, Pursh later lamented, "it vegetated for more than a year, but some accident befalling it, I had not the pleasure of seeing it to flower."

Pursh spent a year and a half with McMahon in examining, describing, and sketching the Lewis and Clark material, with the ostensible aim of preparing illustrations for Lewis's own account of the expedition. Tragically, Lewis never satisfied this assignment of Jefferson's; he died in 1809, a likely suicide. The following year Pursh left Philadelphia taking his notes and drawings and a portion of the Lewis and Clark herbarium with him (the bitterroot collection, minus the rootstocks, which had been planted, remained with McMahon). Pursh settled in London in 1811. As a result, Lewis's account (completed by Clark and others) was published in 1814, without botanical illustrations.

By coincidence, Pursh's *Flora Americae Septentrionalis* also appeared in 1814; it included accounts of about 150 of the plants collected by Lewis,

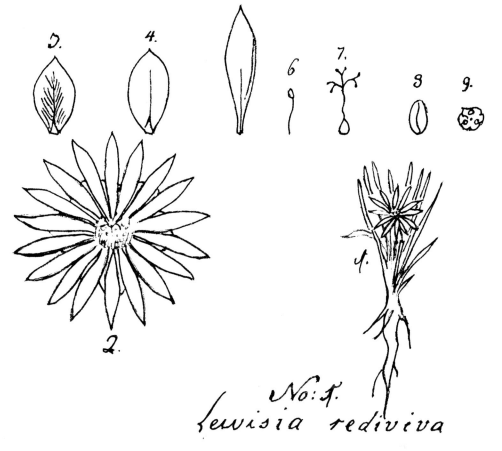

Lewisia rediviva, unpublished illustration by Pursh, 1808(?)

together with the illustrations missing from Lewis's book (*Lewisia rediviva* was not one of those pictured). Pursh's book also included a record of more than forty collections of John Bradbury, made partly in the company of Thomas Nuttall out of Saint Louis.

Pursh (1814) honored Lewis posthumously by giving his name to a new genus of plants, calling the bitterroot *Lewisia rediviva*, meaning "restored to life," a reference to the manner in which the apparently lifeless roots had sprouted in McMahon's nursery. Clark was similarly commemorated in a new genus based on the "most beautiful" *Clarkia pulchella*.

Botanists of the time were not of the same mind regarding Pursh's newly established genus. Thomas Nuttall wrote in 1818 that *Lewisia* was "considerably allied with *Sempervivum*," while William Jackson Hooker maintained in 1833 that, with its inadequately terse description, the genus was "unclearly characterized" and in his opinion "probably merged into *Talinum*." He had of course not seen the fresh flower, nor for that matter had Pursh. Nuttall also carped at the lack of any illustration of so interesting a subject while a lowly lupine and a mundane monarda had been dutifully figured by Pursh. Such an illustration, life-sized and in full color, from a specimen taken by David Lyall, was at last provided in *Curtis's Botanical Magazine* in 1863.

The unusual circumstances that brought forth the specimen portrayed in *Curtis's Botanical Magazine* were cause for great curiosity. Hooker had previously written that herbarium material of *Lewisia rediviva* habitually put out its annual growth for two or more seasons. It was for this reason perhaps that David Lyall, a Royal Navy surgeon who collected plant specimens as he surveyed the United States–Canadian border in 1860, boiled his collections. A year and a half after Lyall collected herbarium material of *L. rediviva*, the plant matter made its way to the Royal Botanic Gardens, Kew, outside London, where the roots soon began showing signs of life, despite Lyall's precautions. Following McMahon's example, a plant was revived and coaxed into bearing beautiful rosy flowers. Walter Hood

Lewisia rediviva by Walter Hood Fitch, from *Curtis's Botanical Magazine,* 1863

Fitch, probably the most celebrated of the early Curtis artists, was assigned to portray the plant. His magnificent painting of bitterroot was the source of much excitement and was cause to forget that Pursh had described Lewis's original flower as white! Now *L. rediviva* was no longer just a name to most botanists; it had been restored to life!

After Pursh (1814) published his description of *Lewisia rediviva*, the genus remained quiescent in the literature until W. J. Hooker and G. A. W. Arnott (1839), unconvinced that *L. rediviva* was a portulacad, established a new but shortlived family, Lewisiaceae, in their *Botany of Captain Beechey's Voyage*. In 1838 John Torrey and Asa Gray began the serial publication of their *Flora of North America; Lewisia* was included in their treatment of the Portulacaceae (Torrey and Gray 1840, 677–678).

Explorers and field botanists, however, soon added more *Lewisia* species; one of them, Sereno Watson, wrote the first manual of Great Basin flora (Watson 1871). By the 1880s botanists started debating the position of this array of new plants in a systematic way. Preliminary to his forthcoming *Synoptical Flora of North America*, Gray (1887) presented a revision of the Portulacaceae that considered *Lewisia* a monotypic genus (comprising only *Lewisia rediviva*); the rest of the newly discovered plants he placed in section *Pachyrhiza* of the genus *Calandrinia*.

A major step in classification was Thomas Jefferson Howell's 1893 publication of a new genus, *Oreobroma* (Greek, neuter, for "mountain food"), to which he transferred Gray's section *Pachyrhiza* of *Calandrinia*. Howell's proposal was controversial throughout its tenure. Mary Katharine Brandegee (1894) succinctly pointed out its ambiguity, and Benjamin L. Robinson (1897) transferred *Oreobroma*, as a subgenus, into *Lewisia*, transforming Gray's monotypic genus into one of eight species; he added another by bringing in *L. triphylla* from *Claytonia*. All the same, Howell's classification had its adherents and was discarded only piecemeal, appearing in the literature as late as the 1950s.

The early years of the twentieth century brought a blow to botanists: despite the heroic efforts of curator Alice Eastwood, who entered the condemned building and lowered some fifteen hundred type specimens by rope to the street below, many type specimens were destroyed when the herbarium of the California Academy burned in the San Francisco earthquake and fire of April 1906, including those of *Lewisia*. That same year, Per Axel Rydberg (1906) created a new genus, *Erocallis*, consisting of a single species, *Erocallis triphylla*. A landmark in western botany was the publication of the first volume of Willis Linn Jepson's *A Flora of California* (1914, 475–480). Rydberg (1932) stubbornly resisted Robinson's transfer of *Oreobroma* to *Lewisia*. More changes in nomenclature were suggested by Sampson Clay (1937), but they did not adhere to the strictures adopted in 1935 by the International Committee on Botanical Nomenclature. Nonetheless, Clay's recognition of the genus's horticultural value was a stimulus to cultivation and further exploration.

Publication was sparse during and following World War II. Exploration was waning, revision on the rise, and yet some lewisias remained to be discovered. In his horticultural monograph of the genus for Britain's Alpine Garden Society, Roy C. Elliott (1966) treated sixteen species, "abid-[ing] strictly by the views of the Liberty Hyde Bailey Hortorium of Cornell University." These he informally disposed into three natural groups, according to growth habit; the second edition of Elliott's monograph, published in 1978, was richer by two species—one discovered only in 1969 (*Lewisia serrata*) and the other, "the *L. pygmaea* of horticulture," welcomed back after decades of "loss" (*L. longipetala*).

Brian Mathew, the widely respected plantsman and taxonomist who was for many years principal scientific officer at the Royal Botanic Gardens, Kew, in England, wrote *The Genus Lewisia* (1989), a monograph that addressed both the classification and the cultivation of these plants. He set up a system of sections based on criteria more sophisticated than that used by Elliott (1966); Mathew's sections form the basis for later discussions of the genus.

The genus *Lewisia* has attracted the attention of several American botanists. Mark Hershkovitz worked during the 1980s and early 1990s on a broad range of the Portulacaceae. Using modern statistical sampling techniques, he revised several genera, particularly *Calandrinia* and *Montiopsis*, and transferred *Lewisia tweedyi* into his reconstituted genus *Cistanthe* (Hershkovitz 1990).

Sean Hogan, while on the staff of the University of California Botanical Garden, Berkeley, amassed a representative collection of live plants and made many field trips, resulting in range extensions and the expected publication of new varieties of *Lewisia cantelovii*. Hogan and Hershkovitz coauthored the section on *Lewisia* for the forthcoming *Flora of North America*, prepared under the aegis of the Missouri Botanical Garden. Some of their findings have been communicated to me in an informal way, and I pass portions of their proposed reclassification along to the reader likewise.

The story of *Lewisia* classification is still unfinished. There are problems to be sorted out concerning natural hybrids; and despite almost two centuries of exploration, the vastness of the American West may still hold lewisias yet unseen by botanists. New taxa continue to turn up, stirring renewed interest in the genus among both scientists and gardeners. One thing is certain: this group of plants is now held in the highest regard wherever discriminating plantspeople are found.

CHAPTER TWO

Lewisias and the Land

MOST simply stated, lewisias are plants of the North American West. From the botanist's point of view, this continent is cleaved into western and eastern portions—but not by the commonly cited geographical feature of the Mississippi River, nor by the Rocky Mountains, nor by the conventional 100° west longitudinal meridian. Rather, Claude Barr, the great plant explorer of the northern Great Plains, identified the eastern edge of the Plains as approximating the 1800-foot (550-meter) contour line at midcontinent; for Barr, everything toward the sunrise from that line was the East, and everything toward the sunset the West, no matter what direction their waters flowed.

If we superimpose this contour line on a map showing average annual rainfall, we see that precipitation to the west of the line, in most places, averages 20 inches (50 cm) or less, all the way to the mountain barrier of the Cascades and Sierra Nevada. Thus the intermountain West is defined as semiarid to arid—a climatic regime that never occurs in eastern North America and northern Europe.

Naturally, in such a vast region, innumerable climatic variations occur, both major and minor. Between the Pacific Ocean and the Sierra-Cascade ranges the climate is characterized as Mediterranean, with moist, cool winters and hot, dry summers. At low to middle elevations there may be no frost until November (and none at all in coastal areas). Nevertheless, arctic air from the Gulf of Alaska or northern interior periodically brings severe freezing as far west and south as southern California; such a calamitous freeze occurred, for example, in 1990.

The intermountain region is of course more continental in climate, although it is affected to a degree by warm, moist Pacific air masses, which push inland and affect the weather in both predictable and unexpected ways. High in all the western mountains, summer thunderstorms are frequent.

The seasonal contrasts of hot and cold or wet and dry are most obvious in the southwestern sector, but there are no absolute climatic boundaries in the West. Influences are continuous and interactive eastward to the Continental Divide on the Rocky Mountains and northward to the buffering ranges of British Columbia.

The interaction of atmospheric movement and surface topography—that is, mountains and valleys—has resulted in distinct climatic and vegetation zones at various elevations. Where precipitation is sufficient, valleys are forested; where not, valley floors are occupied by prairies or deserts. Adjacent to this zone lies a dry mid-elevation steppe characterized by sagebrush, mesquite, manzanita, and cacti, the plants that to outsiders seem to form most of the stereotypical vegetation of the West. Above the steppe the greater availability of moisture from snowmelt usually permits a forest zone. The transition between forest and steppe may be so abrupt that it is often difficult to believe the trees have not been logged off the steppe. This strip between the double treelines is the habitat favored by lewisias.

In the narrow Pacific maritime strip, dense summer fog regularly blankets the coastal mountains from southern California to Canada. This extra source of moisture cools coastal cities in summer and encourages the growth of the redwood forests; it also bars lewisias from this strip, except in the northern extremes of Oregon's Coast Range, the Olympic Mountains of Washington, and southern Vancouver Island, where the bare summits bask in the sun above the fog and the plants are chill and dry under winter's snows.

Persistent snow cover in winter results in copious meltwater in spring, combined with the rainfall. This regime favors the growth of certain lewisias—*Lewisia columbiana* var. *rupicola* and *L. pygmaea*—and many other succulent members of the family Portulacaceae, including *Claytonia*, *Montia*, and *Calyptridium*.

Summer rainfall in the West is generally undependable outside the high mountains, and its effect is more cooling than wetting. Summer rainstorms are intense and brief, and most of the water evaporates quickly from the parched, sun-heated surfaces. On very hot days precipitation may fall without even reaching the ground, a phenomenon known as virga, with the moisture reabsorbed by the thirsty atmosphere. There are, however, occasional wet, sunless summers, which occur perhaps once every thirty to forty years. In 1993, for example, Pacific fog-belt conditions prevailed throughout the West, especially in the Northwest; dryland crops were damaged, but indigenous plants fared better.

A map of lewisia distribution would seem to imply that lewisias are as common as grass in the West—or at least as common as their frequent companions, the many drought-tolerant conifers that dominate the West's forest cover—but this is illusive. No species of the genus is truly common. Lewis and Clark, almost two centuries ago, happened onto one of the few that have really broad distribution, and even this far-flung bitterroot (*Lewisia rediviva*) is exacting in its needs. The specificity of most lewisias to a particular habitat is one reason many of the species were not among the discoveries of the earliest plant-hunters in the West. Most lewisias demand precise, stable conditions in securely remote sites. Practiced lewisia hunters must study the terrain, climate, and geology before they can predict with some certainty whether lewisias might be present, and if so, which ones. This kind of observation is also indispensable to those who aspire to appreciate these plants in their gardens and propagate them for the enjoyment of others.

Evolution and Distribution

Where did lewisias come from, and when? Such soft plants have left behind only the most meager evidence in the fossil record. Except for traces of pollen, every bit of their tissues has long been recycled. For this reason, speculation about the history of the genus relies largely on its present distribution, for which records exist for just the past century or so—a mere wink in time. Nonetheless, when we combine this synchronic (current) knowledge with facts from the geological record, we can propose some hypotheses.

Ancestral portulacads (members of the Portulacaceae) are believed to have existed on the original Pangaean land mass that broke up to become the world's continents, including North and South America. The Appalachian formation in eastern North America was neither glaciated nor submerged for an almost unparalleled extent of time; as a result, it contains a unique repository of the biota of the northern temperate zone, with analogs especially in eastern Asia. Here portulacads are common, though not very differentiated, with *Claytonia* and *Montia* in the cooler sector and *Talinum* and *Portulaca* to the south.

Western North America did not experience such benign circumstances. Indeed, parts of the West arrived much later, and in bits and pieces, through continental drift, plate tectonics, and volcanic action. Mountains were built: the Rockies by uplift and folding, the Sierra Nevada by uplift and tilting, and the Cascades by volcanism and uplift. Most western ranges were formed in cordilleran chains in a north-south orientation, but some, such as the Siskiyous and Uintas, lie east-west in a transverse position. North-south ranges with their long stretches of similar habitat promoted plant migration to north and south; they typically have rain shadows on their leeward eastern slopes. Transverse ranges often contained moderated microclimates, which encouraged the evolution of plants specialized to take advantage of them, thus encouraging speciation.

Glaciers were formed in the Pleistocene era, and a polar cap of ice, miles thick in some places and times, devastated the northern half of the continent. Valley glaciers clawed at the more southerly mountain chains, as far south as southern California. Louis Agassiz (1877) wrote evocatively of this period:

The long summer was over. For ages a tropical climate had prevailed over a great part of the earth and animals whose homes
are now beneath the equator roamed over the world to the very
borders of the arctics . . . but their reign was over. A sudden intense winter, that was also to last for ages, fell upon the globe; it
spread over the very countries where the tropical animals had
their homes, and so suddenly did it come upon them that they
were embalmed beneath the masses of snow and ice.

When the earth finally warmed millennia later, the glaciers melted and
received. Vast pluvial lakes formed in valleys and lowland basins, overflowing those basins to give rise to great river systems. Massive amounts
of sediment accumulated and moved with water and wind to form a thin
cloak of soil over the devastation. As the climate continued to warm and
became drier, more and more of the land surface was exposed to colo-
nization by plants. This sequence was repeated many times over. For a
while, a mixed forest mantled North America from sea to sea, but with de-
clining precipitation, a short-grass prairie replaced the trees of the western plains, where 20 inches (50 cm) of precipitation, or less, could support
nothing more demanding of moisture.

In the midst of this awesome process, lewisias as we know them were
born and shaped. All the rhythms of the Far West are bottled up in them,
all the sun and winds, the wet and dry, hot and cold, push and pull.

The Snowbed Habitat

Lewisias have been able to survive in the arid West by exploiting as much
moisture as possible during a short growing season. Some species then
pass the long arid season by becoming dormant below the surface; others
remain above ground but conserve moisture in succulent, waxy leaves
and a summer dormancy known as estivation.

Probably the single most significant factor affecting the welfare of lewisias is the snowbed. Both a refuge and a launch pad, this habitat has been

crucial to the survival and dispersal of the genus, and probably to its speciation as well. So critical is this association that few species venture beyond this restricted habitat.

Snowbeds exist wherever winter snow is concentrated by the action of wind. They are frequent on rocky lee slopes of the high plains and mountainsides, particularly at high latitudes and altitudes. This occurs most often in the continental interior, but David Rains Wallace (1983) perceived a parallel in the snow forest of the coastal Klamath Mountains of northern California and southwestern Oregon, a refuge for many relict species of both plants and animals, and where lewisias prosper.

This habitat may appear to be less than hospitable for plant life, since it is subject to both prolonged snowfall and constant icy winds. A closer look, however, reveals a surprisingly favorable microclimate in the sheltered hollows where snow lies longest. Here thrive the small plants that depend on full sunlight and cannot survive on forested slopes. Over time, the unceasing wind has also deposited an accumulation of fine particles of rock, volcanic ash, and organic matter in spots where the air currents are deflected or their velocity abruptly reduced by boulders or similar features. This wind-deposited soil, or loess, accrues from many sources; ash, for instance, comes from Cascade volcanoes, both ancient and recent. Dust funneled by the high winds of the Columbia Gorge has been carried as far as the Bitterroot Range of the Rocky Mountains, more than 500 miles (800 km) in a single flow.

The snow that drifts into sheltered lees is concentrated and compacted by wind and its own weight, so that it does not melt quickly in spring, leaving snowbanks at a time when nearby land is already clear. This snow affords the plants beneath it insulation from penetration by frost, preventing spring cycles of freezing and thawing that would heave small roots from the soil. When it finally melts, it provides life-giving moisture in an environment that is otherwise bleak, frigid, and dry. The air near the surface is cool and humid long after less sheltered sites are dried by sun and wind. As the short summer progresses, the snowbed site dries out to some degree; yet even after the snowbank disappears, its bed tends to remain cooler than surrounding areas into the cool days of autumn.

These snowbeds may be extensive, running below the crest of a ridge or the overhang of a ridgetop snowsill. More commonly, we find them as a series of snowbeds, each one only as large as a modest living-room area rug. These may be connected by snow chutes, along which plants can freely migrate altitudinally.

Snowbed habitat of *Lewisia longipetala,* northeast of Basin Peak and west of Truckee, California SEAN HOGAN

This is the perfect nursery bed for seedlings of many species. Wind patterns tend to drop airborne seeds here, and the forest and brush are kept at bay by the thinness of the soil over the rock beneath and by the abbreviated growing season. Most surviving woody plants are small, such as prostrate willows and ericaceous shrublets. The climax community usually includes small rushes (*Juncus*), perhaps with clumps of evergreen beargrass (*Xerophyllum tenax*) or the broadleaf evergreen *Vaccinium* species and *Paxistima*, all bound together with a carpet of mosses and lichens. With taller plants excluded, such sun-loving herbs as *Montia* and *Lewisia* flourish as well.

Entering the realm of a snowbed is a magical experience. One steps out of the wind as if through an unseen wall, into a serene, balmy secret garden complete with birds, beetles, and butterflies. The alpine blossoms rest on the cool moss in the glow of pale gold mountain sunshine, and the air is filled with the scent of green growth. The frequent visitor to the western mountains learns to seek these refuges, for it is here that some of the greatest treasures are to be seen, particularly among the lewisias of section *Pygmaea*.

A Sky Desert

Where so little precipitation occurs that the benevolent habitat of the snowbed is diminished, a surprising number of lewisias have evolved to exploit one of the most forbidding climatic zones in North America. East of the southern Sierra Nevada and beyond the deeply down-faulted Owens Valley lies another mountain mass, gentler than the Sierra in contour, rising from desert on both sides. The White Mountains run parallel to the Sierra for about 60 miles (96 km), more or less straddling the California-Nevada border and merging into the less prominent Inyo Range to the south. Under stormy skies these mountains assume an unreal, chalky gray appearance, like low clouds; most of the time their rocky peaks— once a prehistoric seabed—loom brilliantly white against a cloudless ultramarine sky.

Precipitation here is about the same as that of the adjacent Great Basin, most of it falling as snow, which is then whisked into crevices and slight depressions. A dearth of streams and springs marks the White Mountains as extremely arid, and the absence of stream erosion suggests that this has long been so.

The White Mountains constitute one of about ninety small mountain masses that offer a migration track for plants between the Rockies and the Sierra. Someone once quipped that these ranges on a relief map looked like an army of caterpillars marching to Mexico. The White Mountains are the westernmost of these ranges and the only one that is not isolated on a broad desert floor derived from its own weathered detritus.

Typical "sky desert": the slopes around Saddlebag Lake, at 10,087 feet (3076 meters) in the Inyo National Forest, receive little in the way of snowfall and yet support many species of section *Pygmaea* JOHN MASSEY/PHILIP BAULK

This range also differs in its composition, being primarily dolomitic limestone.

Three factors limit vegetation here: the high magnesium content of the dolomitic substrate, the extreme aridity, and the intensity of infrared radiation. With all but the most tenacious species eliminated, the White Mountains harbor only about one-third of the diversity found on the alpine heights of the Sierra or Rockies. Some of the species found here occur in tundra elsewhere, but these are not strictly tundra or even cold desert plants. It has been suggested that this environment might be termed a sky desert, not unlike that of Alaska's Brooks Range within the Arctic Circle (Zwinger and Willard 1972).

The observer can rarely detect green vegetation on these fellfields from a distance, or even from fairly close, although on nearby eastern exposures the venerable bristlecone pines hold fast. At first it seems a silent moonscape, but on the fellfields some diminutive flowering plants manage successfully against the odds. We must search them out on all fours, so well do they blend with their pallid substrate. Their minuscule leaves, often finely divided into thin ribbons, usually bear a camouflage of white hairs or dense scales, which deflect harmful radiation away from vulnerable tissues. Here are tiny species of *Arenaria, Astragalus, Castilleja, Draba, Eriogonum, Lupinus, Phlox, Thalictrum,* and *Trifolium,* along with many grasses and sedges and tiny composites—even a buttercup. Occasionally we are surprised by the small, hard-scaled rock ferns that frequent these southwestern deserts. In contrast to the clear primary flower colors usually seen in alpine plants, these manage only muted hues, as if their very pigments had been ravaged. The flowers, however, may be larger than the green plants that bear them.

It is surprising that among all this hirsuteness, any glabrous plants can survive, but we see the tiny, narrow, smooth leaves of lewisias of section *Pygmaea,* russeted and purpled by natural pigments. *Lewisia glandulosa, L. nevadensis,* and *L. pygmaea* have been reported from the White Mountains, as well as *L. rediviva* var. *minor.* These lewisias survive here by virtue of their narrow, protectively pigmented leaves, combined with the habit of estivating (remaining dormant) over the long summer and thus escaping such ravages as the most severe solar radiation and drought.

The Sierra Nevada

Roy Elliott (1966) referred to Yosemite National Park in the Sierra Nevada of California as "The Home of the Lewisias, for no less than six species are found within its borders and a seventh just outside." In all, about a dozen of the genus's twenty-seven taxa occur within the Greater Sierran Floristic Province, which includes the foothills as well as the towering peaks of this great mountain chain. The Sierra extends from the Cascadian Lassen Peak in the north to the transverse Tehachapi Range in the south. Although not easily seen, the divergence of the Cascades and Sierra Nevada approximates the North Fork of the Feather River, flowing generally southward more or less along the pre-Cascadian bed of the Klamath River. Its vast uptilted block, about 400 miles (640 km) long and 50 to 80 miles (80 to 130 km) wide, is composed principally of granite, with occasional basalt and serpentine, and an overburden of dark metamorphic rock in the northern portion. During the last ice age much of the Sierra was deeply glaciated, but the highest spires and plateaus escaped as nunataks, offering refuge to alpine plant species.

Most moisture in the Sierra falls as snow in the cold months, and the summers are parched, although thunderstorms occur at higher altitudes. The eastern slope, in the rain shadow, is even drier than the western slope. Snowdrifts may persist most of the summer at the highest elevations, creating the aforementioned snowbed habitat. A few small valley glaciers persist, with associated gravelly moraines and year-round moisture.

All sections of *Lewisia* are present in the Sierran flora. The little carpeting *L. triphylla* of section *Erocallis* occurs widely in vernally wet woodland and other seasonally moist sites, often in great numbers, especially in snowbeds. This tiny plant with whitish or faintly pink flowers is easily overlooked because it is both precocious and ephemeral.

Section *Lewisia* is represented by the bitterroot, *Lewisia rediviva*, particularly in its smaller phase, *L. rediviva* var. *minor*. In the Sierra the bitterroot dwells mainly in the foothills. Related to it is *L. disepala*, seen on the granite screes near Yosemite Valley by hikers who arrive early, while the snow is still on the slopes.

The Sierra flora includes about half a dozen taxa of section *Pygmaea*. California botanists have traditionally separated *Lewisia pygmaea* and *L. nevadensis*, even though populations outside the state, particularly in the north, are not so readily separable. Within the high cirques and adjacent nunatak plateaus, the tundra supports the tiny, brightly pink-striped variant of *L. pygmaea* first known as *L. sierrae*. Nearby, especially on unglaci-

The granite domes, ridges, and screes of the Yosemite region support *Lewisia disepala* SEAN HOGAN

ated plateaus, grows the equally tiny *L. glandulosa,* by some considered a subspecies of *L. pygmaea. Lewisia longipetala* occurs in the northern central Sierra at considerable elevation, confined to the Tahoe Basin, often with two or three other members of this moisture-loving section. *Lewisia kelloggii* is the most distinctive of this section in the Sierra; *L. brachycalyx* and *L. oppositifolia* do not occur within the Sierra, but only south and east, and north and west of it, respectively.

Lewisia cotyledon, namesake of section *Cotyledon,* does not actually enter the Sierra; *L. cotyledon* var. *howellii,* however, grows between Mount Shasta and Mount Lassen in the McCloud and Pit river canyons. In a high, remote basin in Fresno County in the central Sierra there exists a sizable oddly disjunct colony of *L. leeana,* otherwise found only in the Klamath Floristic Province. Nearby, *L. congdonii* is found in infrequent but dense colonies at high elevations just outside the Yosemite National Park boundary and nearby in Kings Canyon. Still farther north, in a few remote Sierra canyons, including those of the Feather River, we find *L. cantelovii* in its variable phases or forms.

The Klamath Region

The northwestern section of California, along with a generous slice of adjacent Oregon, is generally known as Klamath Country. Its major drainage to the Pacific Ocean is the Klamath River, named for one of the tribes of native peoples of the area. This is steeply mountainous terrain with swift and tortuous rivers plunging from the many ranges: the Siskiyous in the north, through the Scott, Marble, Salmon, and Trinity ranges, south to the Yolla Bolly peaks. All these eminences were of spiritual significance to American Indians.

These are not high mountains in comparison with towering Mount Shasta (14,162 feet; 4319 meters), which is visible from most of this region. The crowning glory of the Klamath is Mount Eddy (9038 feet; 2757 meters) at the convergence of the Scott and Trinity ranges, less than 20 miles (32 km) from Shasta across the headwaters of the Sacramento River, which forms the eastern boundary of Klamath Country. Before the terrain was disrupted by volcanism, the waters of the upper Klamath area flowed to the Sacramento to be discharged into San Francisco Bay.

The Siskiyou Range marks the northern extreme of Klamath Country. Its northern slopes drain into Oregon's Rogue River. The range is oriented east-west, with its greatest elevation at Mount Ashland (7523 feet; 2295 meters), the "Grizzly Peak" of early explorers, with permanent snowbeds on its north face. The Siskiyou is the best-known range in Klamath Country among plant lovers and its name is frequently extended to cover the whole region. We often hear, for example, that *Lewisia cotyledon* comes "from the Siskiyous," but that is not the whole story; it also grows in the other Klamath ranges, both within Siskiyou County, California, and both east and north of it.

When the California gold strikes were running out, the Hudson Bay

Klamath Country: Mount Ashland in Oregon's Siskiyou Mountain Range is prime *Lewisia leeana* habitat SEAN HOGAN

trail and the railway and roads that followed it connected California with new gold-mining areas in Oregon and elsewhere. Along this path botanists came to search for new plant life, and four lewisias were found in the Siskiyous alone. This merely hints at the region's botanical richness. The flora of Klamath Country is very old and has been relatively unchanged much longer than that of nearby regions. Here lewisias are happily at home, as are conifers: a single small tract in the Marble Mountains, for example, holds seventeen species of conifers. With great insight, David Rains Wallace (1983) wrote hauntingly of these natural riches—from newts and salamanders to birds, trees, and flowers.

Northern Extremes

At least six species of *Lewisia* have been found in Canada, and one in Alaska. The flora in northwestern Canada is remarkable for its youthfulness, having been reestablished since the last retreat of the Wisconsin glacial ice sheet. Except for the genus *Montia*, the Portulacaceae are not well represented here; the Queen Charlotte Islands, for example, host three species of *Montia* but no lewisias. Three species of *Lewisia* appear to be fairly well represented in southwestern British Columbia, and three others have been reported; all lewisias are protected plants in Canada.

Lewisia columbiana, the typical species of the rainy Northwest, was found in the Ashnola Hills (adjacent to Cathedral Provincial Park) in 1860; it is infrequent in the southern Cascades of British Columbia. *Lewisia columbiana* var. *rupicola* has been known from the highest peaks of Vancouver Island since 1887.

Lewisia pygmaea is occasional throughout much of coastal British Columbia. It also ranges east barely into Alberta and north to Mount McCallum near Atlin, as well as further north into Alaska and the Yukon Basin. *Lewisia triphylla* has recently been reported in southern British Columbia, but only very occasionally so.

Lewisia rediviva was also found as early as 1860 in the dry belt of the Okanagan and Kootenai valleys of British Columbia, two long glacial trenches with extensive moraine deposits draining south to the Columbia River. In 1985 it was reported west of Pincher Creek in southwestern Alberta.

The northernmost known site for *Lewisia tweedyi* is Manning Provincial Park in southern British Columbia. It was confirmed there in 1974 by C. C. Chuang (*Syesis* 7:259) as being "almost white." The claim—repeated by several authors—that it was found in the so-called Wallathian (or Wallachim) Mountains seems to be spurious: there is no record of a range by this name, but L. E. Taylor (1951) did mention "a chalet on top of the mountain pass," a probable reference to the Manning Park highway.

Southern Extremes

Broadly discontinuous populations of species are quite common in the genus *Lewisia*. Curiously, many of the southernmost colonies coincide with disjunct populations of *Iris missouriensis*, suggesting that the two may have shared some past geological and migratory patterns. We find the iris and *Lewisia nevadensis* at Big Bear Lake in the San Bernardino Mountains of southern California and near the summit of Mount Pinos; and *L. brachycalyx* on the mountain ridge of central Arizona, at Lake Cuyamaca in San Diego County, and even in Baja California, Mexico; and *L. rediviva* at Mount Pinos in the Coast Range of Los Angeles and Ventura counties.

It would be fascinating to hunt for lewisias in the most disjunct site of *Iris missouriensis*, more than 800 miles (1285 km) from its nearest present station. This site was discovered in 1860 by the plant explorer Edward Palmer. East of Saltillo in the summit of the Sierra Madre Orientale, due south of Monterrey, Mexico, Palmer came upon a flora that seemed to have been transported wholesale from the central Rockies of Colorado. In 1981, the irises were still flourishing there.

A Lewisia Impostor: *Calandrinia mexicana*

Few other plants have become seriously confused with lewisias in herbaria or in cultivation. An exception is the entity Sampson Clay (1937) discussed as *Lewisia mexicana*. This had been described as *Calandrinia megarhiza* Hemsley 1879 from material taken among the volcanic mountains of Guatemala near its border with Mexico. From another collection, Per Axel Rydberg (1932) described *Calandrinia mexicana*. As many as four other binomials have been proposed, but none was pressed into usage. The names involved combinations of the genera *Calandrinia*, *Lewisia*, or *Oreobroma* with specific epithets *megarhiza* or *mexicana*.

A further source of confusion is the completely distinct species *Claytonia megarhiza*, the taprooted alpine spring beauty of the Rocky Mountains. Several related taxa extend into the Cascade Range north to Alaska.

The Mexican lewisia lookalike occurs from the higher peaks of the central-interior Madrian ranges southward at least into the Central American Talamanca Range, where it persists on glacial cirques of Cerro Chirpino (12,400 feet; 3780 meters) in Costa Rica, and southward into Panama. The plant appears deceptively similar to *Lewisia pygmaea* and like it is capable of growing at subfreezing temperatures. Precocious, solitary, yellow-eyed white flowers, one-half inch (1.2 cm) wide, occur on very short pedicels, huddled among bronzed foliage. It is rarely seen in cultivation.

How Lewisias Travel

Any healthy, vigorous plant—indeed, any healthy organism—naturally aspires to expand its territory. Plant species that do not may be suspected of senescence. The range of a plant (the total area it occupies) is a measure of its relative success in the competitive scheme of nature.

Dispersal of seed is aimed at establishing a plant's offspring in all the places suited to its environmental requirements and tolerances. The genus *Lewisia* has used a number of distinct means of dispersal, not all of which appear to be advantageous under present-day environmental conditions.

Most lewisia seed is merely dropped, and the seedlings may therefore be subject to intense competition both among themselves and with the parent plants. After falling, seed may be further dispersed by the almost constant winds of exposed lewisia habitats; by fall rains and spring snowmelt waters; or by agents such as birds, insects, and animals. The seeds of *Lewisia tweedyi*, for example, are often carried some distance by ants, which seek out warm, dry soil for their nests—the same conditions the plant enjoys.

The seed capsules of the bitterroot, *Lewisia rediviva*, become dry and papery; the wind blows them great distances until they lodge somewhere on the surface, and the seeds drop out. The stalks of *L. cantelovii*, *L. leeana*, and *L. stebbinsii* also separate from the plant in their entirety to be swept across the bare slopes. Little heaps of these strawlike inflorescences, sometimes with seeds intact, can be found in wind-sheltered bays on ridgetops, where they have been carried by updrafts and dropped in lees beside rocks or conifers. Downslope, among the thick trees, a lewisia seedling would have the survival chances of the proverbial snowball in hell.

The leaves of *Lewisia kelloggii* dry up into tight little mopheads in summer, tightly concealing the small, nearly stemless seed capsules. Rodents dig up the roots for food, and the seed is left to reestablish the plants in the disturbed soil. I have recovered seed still so encased that must have been at least two years old.

Seed capsule of *Lewisia rediviva*
BURL MOSTUL

Some lewisias, especially *Lewisia pygmaea* and its relatives, seem to get around superbly though mysteriously. They appear to succeed through sheer numbers and specialized tactics. One mystery is how *L. longipetala*, locked in the most severe snowbed habitat on high ridgetops and surrounded by dry scree, is able to reestablish enough seedlings to survive. We must remember, however, that at some remote time these sky-islands were undoubtedly interconnected, that disjunct distribution is often a remnant of an ancient and extensive unitary population. The wide discontinuities now present in the genus *Lewisia* did not occur overnight; subtle, unrelenting change is a constant force in nature, although it does not necessarily benefit all organisms.

Range extensions are reported for one or another lewisia almost every year, owing more to the energy of plant explorers rather than to the enterprise of the plants. It is highly unlikely that any species is very actively expanding its range at this time. *Lewisia rediviva*, however, is suspected of doing this toward the east—although no one has speculated on its mileage advance per century.

CHAPTER THREE

The Family and the Plant

*T*HE GENUS *Lewisia* belongs to the rather small and distinct portulaca (or purslane) family, technically known as the Portulacaceae, which was established by the insightful French botanist Bernard de Jussieu (1699–1776) and published by a nephew, Antoine Laurent de Jussieu (1748–1836) in his *Genera Plantarum* (1789). This family is widely dispersed: it is especially prominent in western North America, the Andes of South America, and southern Africa; present in Australia, New Zealand, Kamchatka, and Madagascar; and just barely represented in Eurasia. Most portulacads occupy temperate to subtropical regions, but some are found in cooler arctic-alpine zones in the Western Hemisphere. They are typically succulent xerophytes (plants living in dry areas), adapted to near-desert or seasonally dry conditions. Most are small, even inconspicuous herbaceous plants, but the subshrubby *Talinopsis* and even a small African tree, *Portulacaria* (elephant bush) are sometimes grown in warm gardens.

It had always been easy to determine what does and what does not belong to the Portulacaceae. Members of this family are recognized by a unique floral structure. From an apparent calyx (or pair of green sepals) there emerges a corolla-like arrangement of five to many segments enclosing both stamens and pistil. Some botanists regard this as a uniseriate involucre; the green pair of organs are therefore bracts, and the apparent corolla is a perigone of tepals. For practical purposes, however, the calyx of a pair of sepals is considered to support a corolla of petals, to use terms more commonplace. The flowers are regular and perfect, with stamens in multiples of five and a unilocular ovary with campylotropous ovules from a basal central placenta. Dehiscence (release of seed) is variable.

There are about twenty genera in the Portulacaceae, comprising about four hundred species disposed among seven tribes. The genus *Lewisia* constitutes one of these tribes.

Botanists see the Portulacaceae as part of a broader complex, the order Caryophyllales—a diverse lot that includes cacti, pokeweed, *Dianthus*, and *Chenopodium* (goosefoot). All lack the usual anthocyanin pigments of photosynthetic plants, which are replaced here by nitrogenous betalain pigments. They also share certain morphological characteristics, such as having a generally succulent appearance.

Although it contains some plants used for food, the portulaca family is most prized for the many colorful flowering plants useful in horticulture. Notable among these are the North American genera *Claytonia*, *Talinum*, and our subject, *Lewisia*. The South American genus *Calandrinia* too includes some handsome rock garden plants; it is unfortunate that some careless and irresponsible taxonomic decisions of the past century have so confused this genus, which like the camel appears to have been formed by the actions of a blind committee.

The first North American portulacad identified was *Claytonia virginica*, described by the Dutch botanist Jan Frederik Gronovius (1686–1762), who named it for its collector, John Clayton. Clayton, a British colonist in Virginia, supplied most of the specimens used by Gronovius in his *Flora Virginica*, one of the earliest treatments of American plants.

Undoubtedly the most cosmopolitan and edible member of the family is *Portulaca oleracea* (purslane), long a weed of cultivation. Its

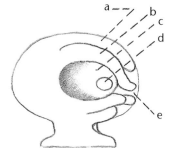

Campylotropous ovule (after Lawrence 1951): outer integument (a); inner integument (b); nucellus (c); egg (d); and micropyle (e)

place of origin is uncertain but probably Mediterranean. A favorite in Mexican and Italian kitchens and a staple of warm-climate gardens everywhere, it is often cooked with eggs and other summer vegetables, as in a fritatta. A variant with thinner leaves has been developed as a summer annual with starry bronze or amber flowers. Another annual, *P. grandiflora*, is cultivated for its brilliant flowers in a wide range of colors.

Another edible annual portulacad is *Montia perfoliata* (miner's lettuce), popular in the gold camps and homesteads of the West and a first-rate spring green when wilted in hot bacon grease and tossed with vinegar and a trace of sugar. The tuberous roots of some *Talinum* species in the Southwest were eaten baked, and the succulent corms of *Claytonia* were choice foodstuffs for Plains Indians and the native tribes of Alaska, who also relished the early leaves of *C. sibirica* after the winter subsistence on blubber. As Lewis and Clark noted, *Lewisia rediviva* was a food source for the Indian nations of the American West; probably all lewisia rootstocks are at least technically edible.

Now that we have met the family, so to speak, let us focus on the individual that most concerns us. Lewisias are small to medium-sized, succulent (thick-leaved), glabrous (smooth-surfaced), perennial herbs. Each species is defined by its own particular combination of characteristics, which together produce the individual phenotype or "look"—as opposed to the genotype, the sum of inherited characteristics. Through the process of natural selection, the genetic constitution of one population may come to differ from other populations of the same species, but only in small respects. By considering the parts of the lewisia plant, we will learn terms that will be useful in distinguishing among the species.

Rootstock

Lewisias are low and leafy. They are usually rosulate (that is to say, they form rosettes of leaves); these rosettes may be simple (one rosette), or there may be a cluster of them, with annual flowering shoots among the leaves. All the rosettes of a single plant are produced from one thickened taproot; this often branches into secondary roots, but in some species (*Lewisia pygmaea*, for example) it is solid, like a little carrot. The taproot and secondary roots produce a delicate web of fine feeding roots that draw moisture from the soil. At the top of the rootstock is a thick neck or caudex, the persistent part (perennating body) of the plant. The caudex, if exposed by erosion, can produce adventitious growths that develop into rosettes; these may later be buried by detritus accumulating around the crown, so that a single plant appears to be a cluster of plants.

Leaves

The foliar parts of a lewisia include bracts and leaves, both of which consist of blade, petiole, and a pair of stipules at the base. Bracts are almost all blade, and the stipules may be minute or absent. Both bracts and leaves are succulent and can shrink in dry periods, looking nothing like their former turgid selves but still maintaining the function of photosynthesis. This ability to change can be exasperating in the field, because the details of bracts and leaves are critical to identifying species. Some species hold their foliage through the year; some are summer-dormant (section *Lewisia*), and others are winter-dormant (section *Pygmaea*).

Most lewisia leaves are plane-bladed (flattened), but some are swollen to cylindrical or terete forms, oval to round in cross-section (as in *Lewisia leeana*). In most species no distinct petiole occurs, but in all a pair of stipules is carried at the leaf base, visible only when the leaf is tugged gently away; the stipules apparently function to protect the growing point, which they surround snugly. The foliage comes in various shades of green, from the almost colorless (hyaline) leaf bases to an intense reddish or purple flush on plants exposed to strong sunlight. In some species, particularly *L. leeana*, the foliage may be pruinose or glaucous, or at least glaucescent (bluish or grayish). The green foliage of *L. nevadensis* has a markedly fresh yellowish hue.

For the most part the leaves are functional, plump, and plain, but a few have interesting marginal features, and since these are among the evergreen species, they appeal to gardeners. *Lewisia cotyledon* var. *howellii* was the first fancy-leaved lewisia to become familiar; its leathery leaf has a fluted, piecrustlike margin as crisp as a cucumber, and with the same cool color contrast. *Lewisia cotyledon* var. *heckneri* has flatter leaves, their margins bristling with fleshy teeth, like a sawblade. *Lewisia cotyledon* var. *fimbriata* manages to be both fluted and toothed. Even more extravagantly dentate are forms of *L. cantelovii*, and *L. serrata* has teeth upon teeth. Cultivated populations of *L. columbiana* occasionally display deeply slashed, almost feathery leaves; this phenomenon reappeared irregularly for about ten years in the lewisia collection of Micheal Moshier, among plants that originated from the western slope of the Washington Cascades.

Bracts

The number, size, and shape of the bracts (leaflets on the flower stem) is significant, as is their relative position. In *Lewisia brachycalyx* and *L. kelloggii* one pair is so close to the calyx that they have been mistaken for a second pair of sepals; in *L. rediviva* a whorl of six to nine linear green wispy bracts marks the juncture of scape and pedicel. In a few species (*L. nevadensis* and *L. tweedyi*) the bracts are simple and entire; in others they are erose or distinctly toothed, and the teeth are often tipped with glands. Such glands, a common feature of many western American dryland plants, may function to attract insect pollinators, which have been hoodwinked into thinking the glands are nectaries. In some species of *Lewisia* there is a correlation between the details of sepals and bracts, while in others there appears to be none.

Inflorescence

Two species, *Lewisia triphylla* and *L. oppositifolia*, have leaves and flowers together on the same stalk. In others the inflorescence is leafless, though bearing bracts, with the true leaves in a basal rosette. The inflorescence may be a simple scape with one terminal flower (*L. brachycalyx, L. kelloggii,* and *L. rediviva*); a few-flowered, short cyme or raceme (*L. pygmaea, L. maguirei,* and *L. tweedyi*); or a multiflowered panicle of as many as fifty (or even more) flowers (*L. cantelovii, L. columbiana, L. congdonii,* and *L. cotyledon*).

Flower

Although the flowers of the Portulacaceae are structurally different from other more common flowers, for convenience we call their parts by the common terms: petals, sepals, corolla, and calyx. Each flower is perfect, including both pollen and ovule. Their shape is actinomorphic, or regular and symmetrical (except for *Lewisia nevadensis,* which is subregular). All have the charming airiness of simple things lacking in labored rigidity. They open for pollination only during the brightest, warmest periods on chilly days, and each flower may open for three or more days in succession. The flowers bear nectar and are fertilized by various bees and flies.

In most species the calyx consists of a single pair of foliaceous (leaflike) sepals; there are seven to nine sepals in *Lewisia maguirei* and six to nine sepals in *L. rediviva.* The sepals may show a purplish stain. The details of the calyx are quite consistent within a species, with the exception of the variable *L. pygmaea.*

Some species (*Lewisia cantelovii* and *L. congdonii*) have only five petals; most have seven or eight; and some (*L. rediviva*) have as many as eighteen to twenty. Each species has its characteristic flower shape—a half-open *L. kelloggii* flower looks like a tiny tulip—and each its own colors and color patterns. The corolla is not shed as it fades but wraps the filaments and ovary until the capsule opens; in *L. tweedyi,* however, it is retained for only a short time.

The stamens are generally the same in number as the petals and are borne opposite them, although when there are very many, this may not be readily apparent. Slender, threadlike filaments bearing versatile (movable) anthers stand rigidly erect at anthesis (the initial opening of the flower). They are protandrous; that is, they mature before the flower's stigma, burgeoning with fluffy yellow pollen. Later, when the stigma becomes receptive, the flower's filaments reflex outward to allow insects to enter and cross-pollinate the flowers. The pollen grains of *Lewisia* species differ in size and surface detail.

The single-chambered superior ovary varies in size and shape, from slightly triangular (*Lewisia tweedyi* only) to globose to ovoid or nearly cylindrical. The single, slender style is cleft in its upper portion into three to eight arms or lobes bearing the stigmatic surfaces that receive the pollen. Placentation is columnar (*L. tweedyi* only) to basal. The ovules range from few (*L. leeana, L. cantelovii, L. congdonii,* and *L. stebbinsii*) to two dozen or more (*L. longipetala, L. nevadensis, L. brachycalyx,* and *L. tweedyi*). The capsule is a dry, thin-walled vessel that releases the seed via a circumscissile suture near its base; the top is shed like a little cap. (In *L. tweedyi* this top is cast off piecemeal rather than as a single unit.)

Stamen: filament and pollen grains

The seeds are more or less flattened, lenticular (lens-shaped) to suborbicular, blackish to dark brown, and glossy to minutely pitted. Those of *Lewisia tweedyi* are coarsely pitted and bear a prominent appendage, the strophiole, which attracts ants. Seed can ripen within a flower that is picked fresh, and the seed of

Protandrous flower: first day (left) and second day

some species can remain viable for several seasons in a sealed, refrigerated container.

Chromosome Numbers

The diploid chromosome numbers given here are adapted from Mathew (1989):

Lewisia brachycalyx	$2n = 20$	*Lewisia leeana*	$2n = 28$
Lewisia cantelovii	$2n = 28$	*Lewisia nevadensis*	$2n = $ c. 56
Lewisia columbiana	$2n = 30$	*Lewisia pygmaea*	$2n = $ c. 66
Lewisia congdonii	$2n = $ c. 24	*Lewisia rediviva*	$2n = 28$
Lewisia cotyledon	$2n = 28$	*Lewisia tweedyi*	$2n = 92$

Those remaining unreported are as yet uncounted. To date, chromosome counts for infraspecific varieties have been found to be identical to the species type in every instance.

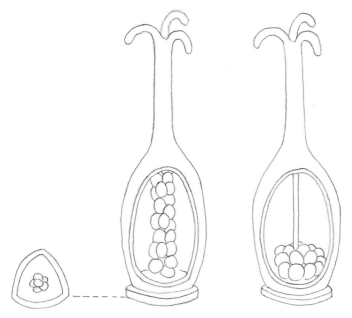

Ovaries: columnar placentation (*Lewisia tweedyi*, left) and basal placentation (all other species)

CHAPTER FOUR

The Species of *Lewisia*

*T*AXONOMIC botanists have subdivided the genus *Lewisia* into several sections, or subgroups, each comprising species that share many characteristics. Not all treatments of the genus *Lewisia* include the same species, nor even the same number of species, because different authors have different opinions of what constitutes a valid species.

In his monograph of the genus, Brian Mathew (1989) presented a more formal infrageneric classification consisting of two subgenera: subgenus *Strophiolum*, with one species, *Lewisia tweedyi*; and subgenus *Lewisia*, with the remaining eighteen species, disposed in six sections. Mathew's suggested classification of *Lewisia* is as follows:

Genus *Lewisia* F. Pursh
  Subgenus *Lewisia*
    Section *Brachycalyx* B. Mathew
      Lewisia brachycalyx
      Lewisia kelloggii
    Section *Cotyledon* J. E. Hohn ex B. Mathew
      Lewisia cantelovii
      Lewisia columbiana
      Lewisia congdonii
      Lewisia cotyledon
      Lewisia leeana
      Lewisia serrata

Section *Erocallis* B. Mathew
  Lewisia triphylla
Section *Lewisia*
  Lewisia disepala
  Lewisia maguirei
  Lewisia rediviva
Section *Oppositifolia* B. Mathew
  Lewisia oppositifolia
Section *Pygmaea* B. Mathew
  Lewisia longipetala
  Lewisia nevadensis
  Lewisia pygmaea
  Lewisia sierrae
  Lewisia stebbinsii
Subgenus *Strophiolum* J. E. Hohn ex B. Mathew
  Lewisia tweedyi

My proposed simplification of Mathew's infrageneric ranking is as follows:

Genus *Lewisia* (succulent perennial from tap-rooted and caudici-
form rootstock, with exception of *Lewisia glandulosa*)
Subgenus *Lewisia*
Section *Cotyledon* (with exception of *Lewisia congdonii*,
  plants are evergreen and dormant through summer; generally broader leaves and taller inflorescences; flowers may be
  large or small)
    Lewisia cantelovii
    Lewisia columbiana
    Lewisia congdonii
    Lewisia cotyledon
    Lewisia leeana
    Lewisia serrata

Section *Erocallis* (globose tuber without caudex; basal leaves
deciduous, replaced by whorl of stem leaves)

    Lewisia triphylla

Section *Lewisia* (plants deciduous in summer with growth
commencing in autumn and inflorescences following in
spring; mature blossoms and seed cast off intact with abscis-
sion in summer)

    Lewisia disepala

    Lewisia maguirei

    Lewisia rediviva

Section *Pygmaea* (fascicled plants deciduous from deep-
seated spring growth)

    Brachycalyx cluster (flowers solitary and sessile, bracts and
    sepals touching)

        Lewisia brachycalyx

        Lewisia kelloggii

    Oppositifolia cluster (pedicels very strongly erect or de-
    cumbent; slight in stature)

        Lewisia oppositifolia

        Lewisia stebbinsii

    Pygmaea cluster (flowers solitary or inflorescences few-
    branched; leaves mostly narrow and channeled)

        Lewisia glandulosa

        Lewisia longipetala

        Lewisia nevadensis

        Lewisia pygmaea

Subgenus *Strophiolum*

    Lewisia tweedyi

A comparison of these two breakdowns shows that I follow Mathew's
1989 classification, except that I propose to transfer his sections *Brachycalyx* and *Oppositifolia* to section *Pygmaea*; I ally *Lewisia stebbinsii* more

closely to *L. oppositifolia*; I treat *L. sierrae* as a synonym of *L. pygmaea*, following Lauramay Dempster (1993); and I accept *L. glandulosa*, which Mathew considers a subspecies of *L. pygmaea* (and which Hershkovitz and Hogan do not plan to evaluate at all). The subgenus *Lewisia* contains basically the same taxa, but I have rearranged them into sections (one with three clusters) that allow a more natural grouping of all the deciduous, spring-emergent species (now together in section *Pygmaea*, except for the cormous member, left in its own section *Erocallis*).

Hershkovitz and Hogan believe that the exact number and limits of *Lewisia* species are uncertain due to morphological variability and intergradation of taxa. They do not identify sections. In any event, everyone agrees that there are about eighteen or nineteen species. In the following account I consider nineteen species, some of them complex. A nontechnical key to distinguishing the sections of *Lewisia* may be helpful:

If the simple, small plant springs from a small, grubby tuber and disappears by summer; and it is found in cool, moist woodlands throughout the range (and it is not a *Claytonia*):

Section *Erocallis*

But if the rootstock is other than a tuber:

And if the compact plant grows from a thickened, plunging rootstock; and it is leafless in the heat of summer:

And if the leaves commence growth in the cool of autumn; and if the flower detaches itself for seed dispersal by wind; and the plant is found in arid, sagebrush steppe conditions:

Section *Lewisia*

But if the leaves do not reappear until spring and the seed is merely dropped locally; and the plant is found in cool, moist conditions, often in tundra:

Section *Pygmaea*

But if the generally larger plant has some functional leaves throughout the year, or nearly so:

And if the thin leaves stand tall, not in rosettes, and are reduced to a green resting bud by summer; and the plant is found on north slopes of the south-central Sierra Nevada in Mariposa and Fresno counties: *Lewisia congdonii*

But if the leaves are thick and spongy, linear to broad or sometimes quill-like:

> And if the plant is a flat, simple, or compound rosette, overtopped by many-flowered stalks; and the seed is revealed when the top of capsule pops off: **Section** *Cotyledon*

But if the leaves mound up on stalks without forming precise rosettes; the large flowers are few per stalk among the leafage; and the seed is dispersed when the capsule breaks into three sections: **Subgenus** *Strophiolum*

Section *Cotyledon*

Most members of section *Cotyledon* are medium-sized to large lewisias, although they do not have the largest flowers. Most are tidy, rosulate plants with generously developed inflorescences. Their flowers may be brilliant, delicate, or as insignificant as those of *Montia*. They can be quite long-lived, developing into impressive clumps. Five of the six species are fully evergreen; the sixth, *Lewisia congdonii*, is summer-dormant in the wild but not necessarily so in cultivation. (The sole remaining evergreen species in the genus, the distinctive *L. tweedyi*, does not belong in this section.)

Most lewisias of section *Cotyledon* can be distinguished on the basis of their foliage, although some knowledge of other features is useful in verifying their identity. Most bear bracts with glandular-dentate margins, but there are noticeable differences in the size and position of these bracts.

Members of this section are found in the mountainous western parts of Lewisialand, from central California north barely into British Columbia (including Vancouver Island). Middle-elevation canyons provide impor-

Middle-elevation canyons, like this one in the Sierra Nevada on the middle fork of the Yuba River, provide important habitat for various species in section *Coty-ledon* SEAN HOGAN

tant habitats for many species in this section, though plants are also likely to be found on exposed ridges and bluffs. Eastern outliers are in the northern Rocky Mountains of Idaho and barely into Montana, all west of the Continental Divide.

A nontechnical key to distinguishing the species of section *Cotyledon* is offered here. It will be useful for identifying plants in the wild but less valuable in dealing with cultivated specimens. One note: wherever *Lewisia leeana* and *L. cotyledon* hybridize to produce *L. ×whiteae*, the hybrid can key out falsely to *L. columbiana*.

If the leaves are thin, flaccid, and erect on obvious tapered petioles, withering while the small five-parted flowers are produced on tall, wispy stalks; and the plant is found only on a few metamorphic ridges in the south-central Sierra Nevada in Mariposa and Fresno counties: ***Lewisia congdonii***

If the leaves are terete to cylindric, oval in section and tapered outward, plump, without a petiole, and prostrate, forming precise evergreen rosettes; and the plant is found on ridges in the Klamath and Siskiyou ranges or high in the Sierra Nevada in Fresno County:
Lewisia leeana

If the leaves are not oval in section, showing distinct upper and lower surfaces, narrow-lanceolate; and flowers are three-quarters of an inch (2 cm) wide or less, with seven to ten petals; and the plant is found in northwestern mountains from northwestern Oregon to Vancouver Island, east to north-central Idaho:
***Lewisia columbiana* complex**

If the leaves are neither narrow nor oblanceolate; the flowers are variable; and the plant is found in the Klamath-Siskiyou ranges or southern Cascades:

And the leaf margins are evenly denticulate to serrate; and small five-petaled pink-veined flowers are borne over a long season on tall, thin indeterminate stalks; and the plant is found in canyons of the northern Sierra Nevada: ***Lewisia cantelovii***

But if the leaf margins are variable; and the larger flowers consist of seven to ten petals, variable in color; and the plant is found throughout the Klamath-Siskiyou ranges north to the Umpqua-Rogue divide of southwestern Oregon and southeast to the canyons of the southern Cascades in Shasta County, California: ***Lewisia cotyledon* complex**

Lewisia cantelovii
J. T. Howell 1942

The ardent naturalists Herbert and Ella Cantelow were descending northern California's Feather River Canyon on 25 May 1941 when they found a lewisia new to them. It bore airy, rose-penciled flowers over blunt leaves margined with soft teeth. It was growing with *Montia*, *Mimulus*, and *Sedum*, tumbling down a towering, wet granite cliff above the roadway and spilling onto the rocky verge. The Cantelows' specimen was brought to John Thomas Howell of the California Academy of Sciences, who published a description the following year, naming the new species in honor of its discoverers.

This lewisia was thought to be extremely local, but in June 1943 more plants were found about 5 miles (8 km) further up the canyon, where they flaunted their flowers from cliffs 200 to 300 feet (60 to 90 meters) above the river. For years, *Lewisia cantelovii* continued to be known as the Feather River lewisia, and unfortunately so. Collectors of the period flocked to the canyon to get their share before it was too late. It was actually possible to gather it in places from a car only by rolling down the window, assuming that one possessed the well-publicized mileage. In no time, the population was depleted; to add insult to injury, the mossy roadside rocks were hauled off as part of a highway improvement project.

Lewisia cantelovii

In recent years, however, the plants have renewed themselves satisfactorily.

The plant now named *Lewisia serrata* is undoubtedly very closely related to *L. cantelovii* and is probably a variety of the Cantelows' lewisia. As this plant has not yet been validly published as such, it would be incorrect for me to refer to it as anything other than *L. serrata*; this situation is likely to change soon, however.

Toothed leaves are not common in the genus *Lewisia*, and those of *Lewisia serrata* are particularly and prominently serrate, with margins like fleshy sawblades, sometimes even with teeth upon teeth. Lawrence Heckard and G. Ledyard Stebbins found this lewisia, with its unusual leaves, in 1969 on the south side of the Rubicon River Canyon, on the western slope of the central Sierra Nevada, to the south of sites for the similar *L. cantelovii*. They published their find as *L. serrata*, noting that it was then known from only three locations (Heckard and Stebbins 1974). Present colonies display a fair degree of variability, but individuals within each colony strongly resemble one another.

It is likely that *Lewisia cantelovii* is a complex comprising all the dentate-leaved evergreen lewisias of the northern Sierra Nevada. There has been much controversy over whether Howell's species should be taken to include certain similar lewisias, particularly *L. serrata* as described by Heckard and Stebbins (1974). In an unpublished letter archived at the Jepson Herbarium, Heckard himself expressed doubts that *L. serrata* is sufficiently distinct to remain as a species. Janet Hohn (1975) proposed that it be transferred as a subspecies of *L. cantelovii*, a suggestion Mathew regarded favorably but without going so far as to adopt it. Hershkovitz and Hogan plan to treat *L. cantelovii* as having three varieties: var. *cantelovii*, var. *serrata*, and var. *shastaensis*.

Lewisia cantelovii: variable leaf margins

The range occupied in present times by *Lewisia cantelovii* in its many variable forms is rather large for its genus, but it is not widespread. The number of known populations is very small—perhaps no more than fifty colonies. Some of these consist of a mere handful of plants occupying a single slope or cliff, isolated by miles from others of their kind in a pattern not unusual for lewisias. Extended isolation and inbreeding have resulted in the distinctive variations that led to taxonomic controversy. In fact, the real differences lie mostly in habitat and leaf morphology; the latter are quantitative, statistical characters, which do not constitute the qualitative distinctions that differentiate valid species.

Lewisia cantelovii is found in one of two habitats: near the rivers, where proximity to misting brings it safely through the summer heat of these canyons, or on cliffside seepages that remain cool all through summer. In any event, it is not tolerant, in nature, to the rays of the intense summer sun. Growth commences as with most of the genus in the coolth of autumn and can proceed through winter; a favored plant may have a froth of blossom for six to eight months. In short, the species is a subject of year-round appeal.

Sean Hogan has grown samples from all known populations of *Lewisia cantelovii* in identical circumstances for comparative study. These plants have stubbornly maintained their individuality, manifesting themselves in forms as different as bold, large, open, tentacular rosettes and soft feathery green cushions, with differing details of dentation. Mathew, viewing this microcosm of the Cantelows' lewisia, commented that it had greater impact than he had been led to imagine.

Hogan's study included material from an unusual colony from a widely disjunct site in Shasta County, extending the range of *Lewisia cantelovii* to the north by almost 100 miles (160 km). This remote and sequestered though still vigorous colony probably represents just one remnant of a species once widespread through the northern Sierra Nevada during interglacial periods. Hogan plans to publish this plant as a new taxon commemorating its existence in proximity to Mount Shasta. It is morphologi-

This canyon wall on the middle fork of the Yuba River in California provides the mossy habitat and shaded rock preferred by seedlings of *Lewisia cantelovii*
SEAN HOGAN

Lewisia cantelovii—the variant that Sean Hogan proposes is a new variety—
Dunsmuir Canyon, Shasta County, California SEAN HOGAN

cally distinguished from the other two varieties in that its sepals are rounded to obtuse (rather than truncate), with irregular, obscure teeth that are not dark-glandular.

Lewisia cantelovii and *L. serrata* share truncate sepals with prominent dark, glandular teeth. Hershkovitz and Hogan intend to differentiate them as follows:

Basal leaves typically red on the underside, regularly and sharply toothed, spatulate, truncate, emarginate, or retuse; pedicels 0.3 to 1 mm; petals elliptic-ovate or elliptic-obovate, 6 to 9 mm long; stems 8 to 16 inches (20 to 40 cm) long; plant found in Nevada, Plumas, and Sierra counties, California (Yuba and Feather river drainages): **Lewisia cantelovii**

Basal leaves coarsely triangular-toothed, oblanceolate to narrowly obovate, rounded to obtuse; pedicels 3 to 8 mm long; petals ellip-tic, 5 to 6 mm long; stems 4 to 10 inches (10 to 25 cm) long; plant found in El Dorado and Placer counties, California (American and Rubicon river drainages): **Lewisia serrata**

To the observer, the leaves of *Lewisia serrata* appear less rounded at the apex; the teeth, often set at right angles to the margin, are much larger and more broadly triangular; the inflorescences are more compact, shorter, and with fewer and less prominent axillary bracts. Plants in the wild appear less robust than those of *L. cantelovii*.

A late-season *Lewisia cantelovii* at Edwards Crossing on the Yuba River in California, its foliage reddened by the summer's heat and drought SEAN HOGAN

A fine specimen of *Lewisia serrata*; note the shorter inflorescences as compared to *L. cantelovii* SEAN HOGAN

The seeds of *Lewisia cantelovii* germinate freely in the mosses that mantle the shaded rocks where it dwells. The few seedlings whose roots penetrate to narrow seams in the rock survive to reach flowering size in a season or two, and any that are fortunate enough to end up on a ledge may attain considerable size and age, as other evergreen lewisias do.

Lewisia columbiana
(T. J. Howell ex A. Gray) B. L. Robinson 1897

Lewisia columbiana is found principally within or adjacent to the Columbia River Basin in the Pacific Northwest. Botanists recognize this as an aggregate of three rather distinct varieties, which grow quite apart from one another along an east-west axis.

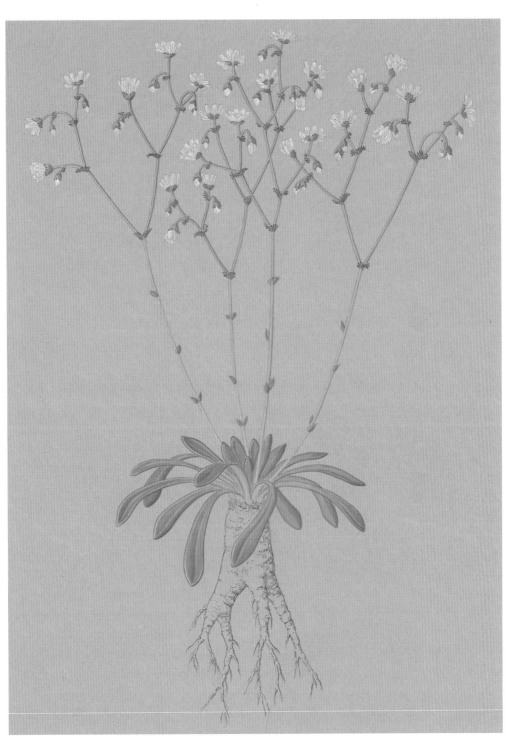

Lewisia columbiana var. *columbiana*

The three varieties of *Lewisia columbiana* are similar in general appearance, except for size. All have narrow, plane-bladed leaves that give an open look to the rosettes; multicrowned old plants can assume a tufted form unlike any other lewisia. Geographically they are distributed across the state of Washington, with outliers in Oregon, Idaho, Montana, and British Columbia, forming a rather tidy pattern of populations on four mainland mountain systems as well as the peaks of Vancouver Island.

Farthest west we find the medium-sized *Lewisia columbiana* var. *rupicola* in the Coast Ranges of northwestern Oregon, the Olympic Peninsula of Washington, and Vancouver Island, extending eastward to the western slopes of the Cascade Mountains in the vicinity of Mount Rainier. The central representative is the type, the larger *L. columbiana* var. *columbiana*, which grows mainly on the eastern slopes of the Washington Cascades from the Columbia Gorge to southernmost British Columbia but also extends south to the Umpqua drainage in southwestern Oregon and east barely into Montana. The third and smallest variety, *L. columbiana* var. *wallowensis*, is found near Hells Canyon of the Snake River, on both sides of the Oregon-Idaho border, to the east across central Idaho, and west barely into northeastern Oregon.

The Columbian lewisias are the northernmost of the evergreen species of section *Cotyledon*. They may be known by their narrowly lanceolate to oblanceolate leaves and slender, ascending bracteate panicles of many flowers. Their petals are commonly seven to nine (but may be as many as eleven), colored whitish to rose to deeper, usually with a vein-pattern of three or more dark lines outward from the base, with many stamens. The ovary is rather cylindrical, the style three-cleft, ovules three to four (or as many as six). Seeds appear a shining deep brown to black.

Hitchcock (1964) determined that the only morphological character (other than size) differentiating the three varieties of *Lewisia columbiana* was the form of the bracts. Unfortunately, these bracts are not very conspicuous even when they are present—and they are not present during a large part of the year. Identification is much aided if one knows the wild

Lewisia columbiana var. *rupicola*

origin of the plant in question. To aid identification, I offer the following nontechnical key to the Columbian lewisias:

If the lowermost bracts of the inflorescence are entire or dentate but never glandular; and the leaves are obtuse to acute at the tips: And the leaves are 1.5 to 4 inches (3.5 to 10 cm) long and no more than 8 mm broad; and the total height of the flowering plant is approximately 8 to 12 inches (20 to 30 cm) or as much as 20 inches (50 cm); and the plant is found mainly on the eastern slopes of the Washington Cascades from southern British Columbia to the Columbia Gorge in Oregon, but disjunct to the Rocky Mountains of northern Idaho or Montana or in the central Oregon Cascades:

Lewisia columbiana var. *columbiana*

But if the leaves are less than 1.5 inches (3.5 cm) long and correspondingly narrow, with pointed tips and lower bracts entire, the uppermost ones dentate but not glandular; and petals are 5 to 8 mm long; and the plant is approximately 4 to 8 inches (10 to 20 cm) in height; and it is found in the vicinity of Hells Canyon of the Snake River in Wallowa County, Oregon and Idaho County, Idaho, and sporadically at summits of highest ridges in Custer, Elmore, Lemhi, and Valley counties on the granitic Idaho batholith.

Lewisia columbiana var. *wallowensis*

However, if the sepals and bracts of the inflorescence are glandular-dentate; and the petal color is whitish to rose to a smoky rose-purple; and the plant is found in the Coast Range from northwestern Oregon to the Olympic Peninsula to Vancouver Island, or on western slopes of the Cascades near Mount Rainier, Washington:

Lewisia columbiana var. *rupicola*

Lewisia columbiana var. *rupicola* can be distinguished from the other two by its bracts, which have toothed margins and are glandular, usually conspicuously so, as are the sepals. The other two differ from each other in scale: *L. columbiana* var. *wallowensis* is far daintier than *L. columbiana* var. *columbiana*, with fewer, shorter, thinner leaves, and the flowers a bit smaller on shorter stalks. The leaves of both *L. columbiana* var. *columbiana* and *L. columbiana* var. *wallowensis* tend to be olive-green and sharply pointed, while those of *L. columbiana* var. *rupicola* are more rounded (or obtuse) at the apex, a little thicker, and deeper green.

In the course of my own fieldwork, I have examined hundreds of wild plants of all three varieties, from the granitic batholith of central Idaho to the basalt peaks of the Oregon Coast Range, from the Okanogan Highlands of southern British Columbia and the peaks of Vancouver Island to the central Oregon Cascades. These wild lewisias were not always what I expected: they ranged from 2-inch (5-cm) rosettes in the easternmost sites to plants in the Washington Cascades that bore 9-inch (23-cm) leaves and bouquets of bloom a yard across, reminiscent of *Saxifraga* 'Tumbling Waters'.

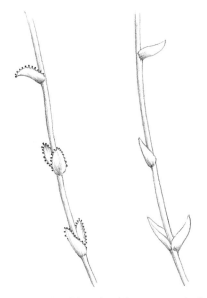

Many populations do not fit convincingly into one of the three varieties. An example is the colony at Granny View Overlook above the steep canyon of the Imnaha River in northeastern Oregon, presumably in the territory of *Lewisia columbiana* var. *wallowensis* (and only a few miles distant from its type station), but including many individuals that are not as neat and tidy as they should be. In the Bitterroot Range of western Montana, near Darby, all the plants in one small colony are as husky as their Cascade counterparts, while a population due south of

Bracts: *Lewisia columbiana* var. *rupicola* (left) and *L. columbiana* var. *columbiana*

there in Lemhi County, Idaho, contains the most diminutive individuals. A colony at High Rock near Mount Rainier would pass for *L. columbiana* var. *rupicola* with sugar-pink flowers, and may indeed be this variety, while another colony, in Oregon's central Cascades, is similar to those found on Vancouver Island.

Lewisia columbiana was one of the earlier *Lewisia* species to become known to science. The Scottish surveyor and naturalist David Lyall, participating in Britain's border expedition of 1860, collected it in the summer of 1860 in the Ashnola Hills of what is now southern British Columbia. These hills are the moraine deposited by the glaciers that sculpted the magnificent mountains of nearby Cathedral Provincial Park. Gray (1887) published the plant as *Calandrinia columbiana*.

Sturgeon Peak provides excellent habitat for *Lewisia columbiana* var. *columbiana* in southwest Washington's Cascade Range SEAN HOGAN

Lewisia columbiana var. *columbiana* is a glacial survivor throughout the Cascades into the Columbia Gorge, where it unaccountably descends from its usual lofty heights to perch on mossy cliffs near streams only a little above sea level, for example in the gloomy slit canyon of Oneonta Creek. More typically, it is found on exposed slopes, particularly near sheltered saddles near mountain spires (which may have protruded from the ice sheet as nunataks, offering a refuge to plant species). It usually grows at elevations of 2000 to 7000 feet (610 to 2130 meters) in the Hudsonian and Arctic vegetation zones. It seems equally happy on whatever substrate is available—basalt, granite, sandstone, or serpentine—and favors deeply subirrigated gritty soils.

In the Cascades, *Lewisia columbiana* var. *columbiana* typically has leaves as much as 6 to 8 inches (15 to 20 cm) long and flower stalks from 8 to 10 inches (20 to 25 cm) in length, rarely to 20 inches (50 cm). The

Lewisia columbiana var. *columbiana* takes in the riparian mist on the bank at White River Falls JOHN MASSEY/PHILIP BAULK

flowers are usually white to blush pink, with a delicate close pattern of rose-cerise veins radiating outward from the base of each petal. A few plants bear completely white flowers. Though not large, the flowers are quite showy. *Lewisia columbiana* var. *columbiana* has outlying populations away from the Cascades, as far as the Bitterroot Mountains of Ravalli County, Montana. Well south of the Columbia Gorge, in the headwaters of the Umpqua River in Douglas County, Oregon, are several small populations isolated from their northern relatives by many miles; these are rather smaller plants and are perhaps more nearly akin to var. *wallowensis* or even to var. *rupicola*.

Lewisia columbiana var. *rupicola*, a lovely claret-flowered plant, has been known since 1915, when M. W. Gorman made collections that are filed in several herbaria. When this plant found its way into cultivation it was for a time known as *L. columbiana* var. *rosea* for its distinctive color. In 1931 Carl and Edith English collected new specimens from Saddle Mountain in the northern Oregon Coast Range. In 1934 Carl English published his Saddle Mountain plant as *L. rupicola* ("rock dweller"). Roxanna Ferris (1944) reclassified it as a subspecies of *L. columbiana*, and Hitchcock (1964) reduced the Saddle Mountain entity to a variety. (Hershkovitz and Hogan too intend to treat it as a variety.) Both morphologically and ecologically, however, *L. columbiana* var. *rupicola* might be considered a distinct species. It is intermediate between varieties *columbiana* and *wallowensis* in size, but in other respects, particularly in bracts and sepals, it resembles *L. cotyledon*, which occurs only much farther to the south. (I am indebted to Janet Hohn for this observation.)

The distinctive dark rose-claret of the form found on Saddle Mountain is thought to be typical of *Lewisia columbiana* var. *rupicola*. Although the venation is not obvious to the eye, it lends a smoky tint to the flowers as they tremble in the breezes of the humid Pacific slope. Other populations of *L. columbiana* var. *rupicola*—in nearby Tillamook County, near Mount Rainier, in the Olympic Mountains, and on Vancouver Island—do not have such dark flowers; some are a lovely rose-pink. Most, however, exhibit the prominent veining typical of var. *columbiana,* and white individuals are occasional. Morton E. Peck called this the rosy lewisia; I prefer calling it the coast lewisia, for its unique humid habitat.

Lewisia columbiana var. *wallowensis* is a diminutive phase of the species. Its range is centered in the canyons of the Snake River and its tributaries, in the ancient region the pioneer geologist Thomas Condon called Shoshone. Early mentions of *L. columbiana* in the "canyons of the Blue Mountains" referred to this plant, although it was not recognized as distinct until Hitchcock (1964) published a description of specimens collected by Arthur Kruckeberg in July 1950 on the Oregon rim of Hells Canyon on the Snake River.

A specimen of *Lewisia columbiana* var. *rupicola,* its flowers slightly paler than the norm, from Onion Peak, southwest of Saddle Mountain BURL MOSTUL

This small lewisia is found on the crests of canyons eroded steeply from this plateauland. Its range extends from the drainage of the Imnaha River, Oregon, in the west, eastward across some of the deepest canyons in North America into the Seven Devils Mountains of Idaho, beyond the equally deep Salmon River chasm, nearly to the Bitterroot Mountains, almost reaching Montana at subalpine elevations. Ironically, *Lewisia columbiana* var. *wallowensis* is not actually found in the Wallowa Mountains, a cluster of upthrust peaks protruding through the ancient plateau; the varietal name alludes to Wallowa County, Oregon.

Variety *wallowensis* is common in ridge-and-brow communities in situations where snow sills lie in winter, protecting the plants against the deep continental cold and providing spring moisture. The lewisias do not descend into the canyons, which become like furnaces in summer. They often produce great sheets of flower on basalt or granite in Oregon or on granite in Idaho.

Lewisia columbiana var. *wallowensis* hails from the highest elevations surrounding Hells Canyon BURL MOSTUL

These same fellfields support scattered yellow, lodgepole, and white-bark pines, larch, and fir; bulbous plants such as *Fritillaria pudica* and the ubiquitous *Allium* species; blue *Mertensia*, violet *Primula cusickiana*, and yellow *Erigeron*. Here too is the diminutive *Penstemon fruticosus* var. *serratus*, which is to its species what var. *wallowensis* is to *Lewisia columbiana*: both are shaped by their habitat to more petite size, with intermediate forms growing nearby in less severe conditions.

Lewisia columbiana var. *wallowensis* has flowers colored and veined much like those of var. *columbiana* in the Cascades. Sometimes its petals are snowy white, which makes an appealing contrast to the cinnabar stamens.

Lewisia congdonii
(P. A. Rydberg) S. Clay 1937

Attorney and naturalist Joseph Whipple Congdon first spotted his semi-deciduous lewisia on 31 May 1883, on rocks in the canyon of the Merced River in the foothills of the Sierra Nevada in California (the species' single known lowland station), at an elevation of 580 feet (175 meters). Congdon was making a botanical reconnaissance of the Yosemite region; although this scenic wonderland was not to be preserved as a national park for many years, it had been a tourist attraction since the mid-1870s.

Later plant-hunters sought this lewisia in vain and presumed correctly that it had gone into summer rest, as so many other western plants did. It was finally found again in 1924, growing alongside a road by the river near Hennessey's Ranch, where the seed had apparently fallen from the rocky ridge above (Hennessey Ridge on current maps). This was the collection described, as *Oreobroma congdonii*, as the type (Rydberg 1932) and reclassified as a subspecies of *L. columbiana* (Ferris 1944).

Congdon's lewisia does not fit the mold for the genus in several respects; at first sight it looks more like a lush montia. Yet *Lewisia congdonii* has an indefinable quality of strength all its own. Many who have sought

Lewisia congdonii

it have failed; those who have succeeded all seem to agree that the plant was mildly disappointing, though they wished to say something nice about it.

Lewisia congdonii is a robust lewisia in all its parts, with a husky caudex that may be more than a foot long. From this rises a multicrowned plant with upstanding mule-ear leaves; these are thin for a lewisia, of a pale, soft, shining khaki-green. In decline the leaves become flannelly and brown as the tissues shrink, until finally the dormant plants blend with the tan Sierra summer landscape.

Several flower stalks, sturdy and indeterminate, occur per crown. The flowers, on threadlike pedicels, are about three-quarters of an inch (2 cm) wide, with six or seven petals of pale pink veined brightly in beetroot-purple; sometimes, however, the effect is merely pastel pink. Each flower has but few ovules, but so many flowers are produced that the seed-set is wondrous. Like *Lewisia cantelovii*, *L. congdonii* can flower throughout the season until frost when constant moisture is available.

A husky specimen of *Lewisia congdonii*, just as Congdon found it, clinging to rocks in the Merced River Canyon, California SEAN HOGAN

Lewisia congdonii is now confined to Fresno and Mariposa counties, California, on the western slopes of the Sierra Nevada, at elevations from 4000 to 9000 feet (1220 to 2745 meters), growing on the metamorphic overmantle of the granite base. This species is common and conspicuous on the few slopes where it persists. A 1978 report considered it for inclusion on the endangered species list, attracting much attention and resulting in the identification of several stable, flourishing colonies, with larger populations numbering in the thousands of individuals. It is presently regarded as rare but not threatened and can be expected to remain in this category as long as its habitat remains undisturbed.

Lewisia congdonii behaves as if it were a relict from a cooler, wetter era, and it looks as if it might have been good fodder for herbivorous dinosaurs! It is certainly no coincidence that it survives in the company of the relictual *Sequoiadendron giganteum* (giant sequoia), as well as such other endemic species as *Allium yosemitense*, *Eriophorum congdonii*, and *Sedum spathulifolium* var. *yosemitense*. Shrubby companions, including *Quercus chrysolepis* var. *nana* and *Arctostaphylos manzanita*, lend cover, while *Streptanthus tortuosus* var. *suffruticosus* and *Selaginella hansenii* dominate the herbage near the lewisias. Twining brodiaea (*Dichelostemma volubile*) and *Calochortus* make occasional cameo appearances as well.

As for growing this semideciduous plant, many plants can be grown quite differently from the way we find them in nature and yet perform very satisfactorily. Floyd McMullen and David Hale have both observed that you could keep lewisias (particularly *Lewisia cotyledon*) literally forever merely by keeping them dry, but if you wanted flowers on them you had to risk giving them water, although this could be their death knell. Hale's approach to Congdon's lewisia was to encourage the foliage to remain functional as long as possible by keeping its habitat cool. He grew *L. congdonii* atop a north-facing wall, where it received a lot of sun but had a cool root-run. One year it might flower to perfection, but the following year perhaps not at all, even with extra water. Could we be asking too much, then, when we hope for an annual show-stopping display?

Lewisia congdonii first flowered in Britain around 1970. Fresh seed I had collected on Mount Trumbull (DHM 89-7, Mount Trumbull) was grown by Tony Hall of Kew; one of the resulting plants won a preliminary award at the 1990 Westminster Spring Show, creating renewed interest in the species. It would be interesting to extend and perpetuate its effect in garden selections.

A thriving station of *Lewisia congdonii* on the bluffs above the Merced River
Canyon in California SEAN HOGAN

Lewisia congdonii in flower at 5400 feet (1650
meters) west of Yosemite SEAN HOGAN

Lewisia cotyledon
(S. Watson) B. L. Robinson 1897

It is not surprising that this extremely variable species has been subdivided into several varieties by various authorities. Hershkovitz and Hogan plan to recognize three varieties: var. *cotyledon* (S. Watson) B. L. Robinson, in which they subsume var. *purdyi* W. L. Jepson and *Lewisia finchae* C. E. Purdy; var. *howellii* (S. Watson) W. L. Jepson; and var. *heckneri* (C. V. Morton) P. A. Munz. Janet Hohn (1975) examined both herbarium specimens and plants in the wild before deciding that there were five distinct taxonomic phases, which she designated subspecies rather than varieties; four were transfers from varietal status, and the fifth was a new taxon, *L. cotyledon* subsp. *fimbriata*. My discussion of the species employs Hohn's scheme but retains the varietal status assigned by other authorities. I offer the following nontechnical key to the five recognized varieties of *L. cotyledon*:

> If the leaves are plane-bladed (flattened) with smooth margins:
>> And the leaves are lanceolate to oblanceolate to narrowly obovate and more than 1.5 inches (3.5 cm) long; and the plant is found on ridgetops widely distributed in the Klamath-Siskiyou ranges: *Lewisia cotyledon* var. *cotyledon*

>> But if the leaves are broadly obovate and less than 1.5 inches (3.5 cm) long; and the plant is found in Curry and Josephine counties, Oregon, in open situations: *Lewisia cotyledon* var. *purdyi*

> If the leaves are not with simple, entire margins:
>> And the leaves are plane-bladed with distinct marginal dentation; and the plant is found in canyons in eastern Trinity County, California: *Lewisia cotyledon* var. *heckneri*

Lewisia cotyledon var. *cotyledon*

But if the leaves are not plane-bladed, margins undulate:

And the leaf margins are not dentate; and the plant is found widely in cool, wooded canyons, not in Trinity County: *Lewisia cotyledon* var. *howellii*

However, if the leaf margins are both undulate and dentate; and the plant is found in canyons of western Trinity County: *Lewisia cotyledon* var. *fimbriata*

The dazzling and puzzling variability of the wild populations of *Lewisia cotyledon* was noted in Elliott's monograph (1966), and Marcel LePiniec (1964) offered this strong caution:

Concerning the so-called species [of *Lewisia*], *howellii, finchae, heckneri, purdyi, longifolia, latifolia, angustifolia,* and all the other-*folia,* I advise gardener and botanist alike against hairsplitting, at least until they've taken a good long look at Louisa's lusty progeny; that so few were christened is the only wonder.

A vast range of cultivated variants, too, are now convened merely as cotyledon hybrids (that is to say, hybrids involving *L. cotyledon*).

Lewisia cotyledon var. *cotyledon* was first collected by Thomas Jefferson Howell in June 1884. As the first member of this complex to be described, by Sereno Watson in 1885, it became the type of the species from the taxonomist's point of view and for everyone's convenience; it may, however, be the most misunderstood of all the varieties. Its main distinguishing feature is the plane-bladed leaf with entire margins, but not all individuals in wild populations conform precisely to this description. Some intergradation may occur among the varieties in northern California and southwestern Oregon, although some colonies are much more isolated and therefore more uniform. Those observed at Devils Punchbowl would seem to be such a colony, although *L. leeana* occurs there, as do the *L.* ×*whiteae* hybrids.

The leaves of *Lewisia cotyledon* var. *cotyledon* are large and broad, usually 4 to 6 inches (10 to 15 cm) long in the wild but capable of reaching 8 inches (20 cm) or more in cultivation. The flowers tend not to be as ample as those of other varieties of *L. cotyledon*; the petals are as variable in size and shape as the leaves. The base color of the flowers is ivory white to creamy yellow, veined along the center of each petal with bright rose or magenta, giving the effect of a child's pinwheel. The veins fade to a muted peach color in certain remote, isolated colonies. The rose color may be only a blush, or may saturate the petal almost completely. In yellow-based flowers the rose veins create a warm copper or orange tone.

Lewisia cotyledon var. *cotyledon* is a denizen of ridges and cliffs, occurring where its top growth receives bright sun but its roots plunge into a cool substrate, usually on a northern exposure. It has been in cultivation since around 1890, when Clarice Paul transplanted a specimen from the nearby mountains into her family's garden in Grants Pass, Oregon; it has been grown abroad since at least 1906, when it first flowered at Kew, and was featured in *Curtis's Botanical Magazine* in 1908.

Lewisia cotyledon var. *heckneri* forms a plane-bladed, flat rosette with leaf margins like fleshy sawblades (a characteristic shared by *L. cantelovii*).

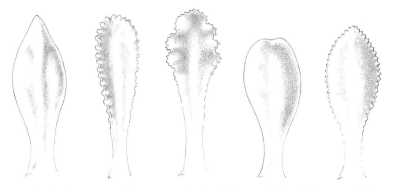

Variable leaf margins of *Lewisia cotyledon*: (left to right) varieties *cotyledon*, *howellii*, *fimbriata*, *purdyi*, and *heckneri*

Prime *Lewisia cotyledon* var. *cotyledon* habitat on Whisky Peak, Josephine County, Oregon PHYLLIS GUSTAFSON

The flowers are usually white with pink stripes; from a distance they may appear pink to rose. It was first recorded in 1930 by the Australian-born plant collector John H. Heckner on steep, mossy canyonsides in northern California above Canyon Creek, a tributary draining from the north into the Trinity River. In 1931 it was described by Conrad V. Morton as *Oreobroma heckneri*, honoring Heckner, who operated a small specialty nursery of native plants; it was transferred to *Lewisia* the following year (Gabrielson 1932). Philip A. Munz (1959) demoted *L. heckneri* to a variety of *L. cotyledon*.

Steven Darington has observed the Trinity River lewisias for many years and mapped their occurrence. He presents a strong case for introgression at certain intermediate stations between the several variants of *Lewisia cotyledon* in the region, proposing that *L. cotyledon* var. *fimbriata* may be ancestral to var. *heckneri*.

Lewisia cotyledon var. *heckneri* on a tuft of moss at Canyon Creek, a tributary of California's Trinity River MARGARET WILLIAMS

Heckner's lewisia is now becoming scarce in its Canyon Creek homeland, perhaps because of overcollection. It is impossible to say how plentiful *Lewisia cotyledon* var. *heckneri* may once have been in the upper Trinity drainage west of Mount Shasta, which was subject to devastating
scouring in the days of hydraulic mining. At one station near Canyon
Creek there is a remnant of what must have been an enormous population before miners removed most of Oregon Mountain to recover its rich
ore, more than a century ago. *Lewisia cotyledon* var. *heckneri* has been in
cultivation in Britain since the early 1930s; it received the Award of Merit
when exhibited by Sir William Lawrence in 1932.

Lewisia cotyledon var. *purdyi* is a taxon erected by Jepson (1914, 475–
480) from material taken in the Illinois Basin of southern Oregon. Jepson
named this lewisia, which is marked by a very compact, caespitose growth
habit, in honor of nurseryman, author, and native-plant enthusiast Carl
Purdy. Because Jepson did not name a type specimen, Hohn proposed to
designate a neotype found at Babyfoot Lake in Curry County, Oregon.

Lewisia cotyledon var. *purdyi*, Fiddler Peak, Curry County, Oregon SEAN HOGAN

Among local wildflower enthusiasts, *Lewisia cotyledon* var. *purdyi* came to be called the button rockrose because of its resemblance to the big fabric-covered buttons on women's coats in earlier days. Its compact habit should appeal to any grower of alpines. The flower colors, which include a yellow like that of butter exposed to the summer sun, are as variable as those of other varieties. The sturdy plants inhabit ridges and fellfields, where they are sheltered and watered by the winter snows but exposed to brilliant sun in summer.

Lewisia cotyledon var. *howellii* was first described in 1888, as *Calandrinia howellii*, by Watson. The name honors Thomas Jefferson Howell, who collected the type plant in 1887 in the Deer Creek Mountains of Josephine County, Oregon. Howell was following a wagon route from the Illinois Basin north to the Applegate River. Willis Linn Jepson (1914), ignoring *Oreobroma*, reclassified it as *L. cotyledon* var. *howellii*.

Variety *howellii* is best known for its intricate rosettes of leathery, crinkled leaves, although not every individual has such amusingly ruffled foliage. The flowers are like those of typical *Lewisia cotyledon* but are usually soft pink. The plants tend to form large single rosettes.

Lewisia cotyledon var. *howellii* is widespread in the wild, extending north into the Umpqua River drainage along Cow Creek in Douglas County, Oregon, and east to the canyons of the Pit and McCloud tributaries of the Sacramento River in Shasta County, California. This variety is a canyonside dweller, seeking cool, stony riparian sites beneath the woodland canopy of low-elevation oaks, where snow may fall but seldom persists for long. The rocky substrate is covered with mosses, which remain dripping wet much of the year but become powder-dry in summer.

Lewisia cotyledon var. *howellii* has given rise to the remarkable cultivar 'Carroll Watson', which was found in the upper Rogue River drainage in Jackson County, Oregon. Marcel LePiniec named it for the man who found it and brought it to him. 'Carroll Watson' received an Award of Merit when shown in Scotland in 1974.

Another taxon, *Lewisia cotyledon* var. *fimbriata*—proposed by Hohn

(1975) as a subspecies of *L. cotyledon* but treated here as a variety, for consistency—was to include those populations in western Trinity County, California, that had leaves both crenulate (or fluted) and dentate (with marginal teeth). This plant appears to be close, both morphologically and geographically, to both *L. cotyledon* var. *howellii* and *L. cotyledon* var. *heckneri*, though distinct from each. (Darington discerned evidence of *L. cotyledon* var. *fimbriata*'s introgression with *L. cotyledon* var. *heckneri*.) Lewisia cotyledon var. *fimbriata* was offered by Carl Purdy from around 1938 to 1940 under the apt name *L. cotyledon* var. *heckneri* 'Elegans'.

Lewisia cotyledon var. *fimbriata* is little known in cultivation (Purdy's *L. cotyledon* var. *heckneri* 'Elegans' apparently never became known in Britain and has been nearly forgotten at home as well). Its flowers cover the full color range of the species, primarily in rosy hues. The vigorous plants of this variety reside mostly on precipitous rock faces in the Trinity River Canyon (but also on low surrounding mountains to the south), where they are watered by both rain and snowmelt. A remarkable albino individual collected by Darington—at the cost of a couple of broken ribs—has been named *L. cotyledon* var. *fimbriata* 'Roy Davidson'; from it, Darington developed a white seed strain and distributed plants to Philip Baulk, of Ashwood Nurseries at Kingswinford in the West Midlands, England, among others. Darington himself still has several dozen of its self-pollinated offspring.

A particularly showy variant of *Lewisia cotyledon* became popular in cultivation, owing in part to its wild occurrence in accessible sites along the middle reaches of the Klamath River and its tributary, the Salmon River. This was the "cliff-maiden" of wildflower writer Dorothy King Young. These wild forms, in the few times they have surfaced, have been allied by some authorities with *L. cotyledon* var. *howellii* and have figured significantly in the development of garden lewisias; many are near duplicates of those identified as *L. cotyledon* var. *howellii* and *L. cotyledon* 'Rose Splendour' in Plate 11 of Mathew's 1989 monograph.

This Klamath form differs morphologically from all other forms of

Lewisia cotyledon in its more funnel-form flowers of bright rose, with petals narrowly banded in paler pink or white. The bases of the petals are yellow, giving the flower a tiny golden eye. The leaf edges are somewhat wavy but not undulate as in *L. cotyledon* var. *howellii*. Uniquely, the style extends beyond the corolla, so that fertilization is possible even when the flower is technically closed. The solid-colored flowers raised by Frederick W. Millard in England could well have originated in part from these "cliff-maidens." 'Rose Splendour', a selection of *L. cotyledon* var. *howellii* raised by A. G. Weeks, was almost certainly from Millard's stock; this named form received the Award of Merit in 1965 and served as a key plant in early breeding in Britain as well as a standard for comparison.

The few known remaining wild colonies of these Klamath lewisias consist of only a few individuals in isolated sites in Siskiyou County, California. The others have been decimated both by floodwaters and by collectors.

In his treatment of cultivated lewisias, Roy Elliott (1966) noted that the garden strains of *Lewisia cotyledon* had become so mixed as to have lost their original identities, the various phases of the species being completely interfertile. Mixing and selecting forms in cultivation results in varying degrees of success. Some strains are more stable, others more variable. Whatever the goal of the breeder—for example, bright color or size of flower—the strain ought to improve from one generation to the next. "We've come a long way," wrote Scotland's Jack Drake of his Sunset Strain, "from the old wishy-washy striped magenta-pink flowers." Indeed, *L. cotyledon* has been made so amenable to commercial cultivation and so showy that garden centers now feature big displays of plants

Lewisia cotyledon var. *howellii*, Klamath River, California SEAN HOGAN

in gallon containers, bursting with flowers in strawberry, raspberry, cherry, orange, lemon, and lime.

A seed strain is different from a clonal cultivar (named variety) in that the latter can be propagated only vegetatively—in the case of lewisias, by detaching side rosettes and treating them as cuttings. A seed strain, by contrast, results from the repeated crossing of selected parents to produce populations of seedlings that predictably share certain desired characteristics. Strictly speaking, the offspring of seedlings of Drake's Sunset Strain, for example, should not be called "Sunset Strain" unless the seed came from Drake's nursery; in practice, however, that name has been applied throughout the trade, whatever the provenance of the plants.

The first reported lewisia seed strain was developed from plants of *Lewisia cotyledon* that were selected by Mary Finch around the Illinois Basin of southern Oregon and brought to the nursery of Carl Purdy, who introduced them as a new (and now invalid) taxa in 1932, *L. finchae*. They were very floriferous, with as many as five hundred flowers per plant. Old-time gardeners still remember "Granny" Finch and her namesake lewisias, although the name tends to be written "finchii" now. One of her great-granddaughters has speculated that Finch's original collections were made around Bolan Lake, which her great-grandmother stocked every spring, while out tending her cattle, with fingerlings she carried in her saddlebags. Many early western nursery catalogs offered these color forms and certainly they were among the first variants of *L. cotyledon* sent abroad in the early twentieth century; *L. cotyledon* var. *howellii* and *L. cotyledon* var. *cotyledon* were also grown widely.

The plants Frederick Millard grew in Britain were significant in that they resulted from a deliberate program of selection. "No plant has ever responded to the camel-hair brush as have the Lewisias," Millard (1935) exulted. "I have succeeded in obtaining rich deep carmine, lovely pinks and several intermediate shades, many of them self-colored, all signs of the stripe having been eliminated . . . to the wonder of all who have seen them."

Millard lived first in the west of Ireland, where he operated an oyster fishery and raised flowers, including lewisias. In 1913 he obtained from Mary White of Waldo, Oregon, a plant of *Lewisia cotyledon* var. *howellii*, poor and shriveled after a long sea voyage, which he soon had flourishing and setting seed. Around 1920 he left Ireland for Camla, at Felbridge in Surrey. At Camla his lewisias grew like cabbages (and his *Nomocharis* like scallions, as Lester Rowntree has observed). Camla plants helped to replenish many nurseries and famous gardens after World War I. The "microspecies" Sampson Clay (1937) referred to as *L. millardii* was probably the result of Millard's work, although Elliott (1966) surmised it was one of Carl Purdy's selections. Stuart Boothman offered it for sale in 1954, praising its "leaves without crinkles and flowers of light pink striped with scarlet."

It is possible that the lewisias of A. G. Weeks of Weald Cottage, Limpsfield, Surrey—only a few miles from Camla—originated from Millard's strain. After twenty years of raising seedlings "from two plants from a friend," Weeks's 'Weald Rose', a selection of *Lewisia cotyledon* var. *howellii* raised in 1948, won an Award of Merit at the 1951 Chelsea Flower Show. All Weeks's subsequent lewisias were derived from it. Weeks wrote that his plants were from a long line of pale pinks, but it was a rose-colored apparition that parented the prizewinner 'Weald Rose', a cherry pink with a deeper stripe; its descendants varied from deep rose to orange to pale yellow. By this time Weeks was also growing Mary Byman's strain of *Lewisia cotyledon*, and bees will be bees.

Another of Weeks's selections was the superb *L. cotyledon* var. *howellii* 'Rose Splendour', which received an Award of Merit on 4 May 1965 when exhibited by Will Ingwersen. In his *Manual of Alpine Plants*, Ingwersen praised 'Rose Splendour' for its masses of rich, clear pink flowers; he noted that "the name tends to represent a seed strain of slightly variable tint," and he offered it as such in catalogs. This cultivar, or strain, had a profound influence on Ingwersen's own Birch Strain, selected for colors of pink, salmon, and crimson, sometimes all combined in a single flower.

Undoubtedly the most widely grown strain of garden lewisias origi nated in Inshriach Nursery at Aviemore, Inverness-shire, Scotland—fondly remembered as Jack Drake's, although it passed some years ago to John Lawson. Drake selected plants of *Lewisia cotyledon* over a number of generations until he was astounded by a small one with brilliant orange-scarlet flowers. Named 'Comet', this was to become the progenitor of Drake's Sunset Strain, which featured flowers in bright lemon, apricot, peach, melon, and bronze tones, as well as pink, rose, and the original scarlet. Now long gone and long eclipsed, 'Comet' was nonetheless a landmark on the lewisia journey.

Other *Lewisia cotyledon* seed strains originating in the British Isles include two whose similar names can be confusing—the Ashmore and Ashwood strains. The Ashmore Strain was developed some years ago by Lieutenant Colonel Stitt of Blairgowrie, Perthshire, Scotland, from the famous lewisias grown by John and Dorothy Renton at their Branklyn Garden in Perth. The more recent Ashwood strains come from Ashwood Nurseries, where they were developed by Philip Baulk; these are noted for their yellows and for the clone 'Ashwood Ruby'. A recent departure is the Ash-

Exceptional double forms developed at Ashwood Nurseries, West Midlands, England, the source of many breeding advancements in *Lewisia cotyledon*
JOHN MASSEY/PHILIP BAULK

wood Carousel Strain, with smaller plants that are quickly and easily grown, offering pastel flowers on short stems.

In North America, Betty Ann Addison of Rice Creek Gardens in Minneapolis continues the work begun by lewisia breeder Carl Gehenio. For nearly two decades and from many seed sources, she has selected plants that retain a single open crown without crowded offsets. This habit, common in the wild, appears to be most tolerant of both winter freezing and summer mugginess. Rice Creek Gardens offers two superior vegetatively propagated selections of *Lewisia cotyledon* adapted to the bitter winters and hot, humid summers of the central and northeastern states: 'Candy Cane' (with candy-striped flowers) and 'Ruffled Ribbons' (with pure pink flowers and distinctly crinkled foliage).

Lewisia leeana
(T. C. Porter) B. L. Robinson 1897

Lewisia leeana was first collected by Lambert Wilmer Lee, a member of the party of the U.S. Geological Survey that fixed the border between California and Oregon, on 2 August 1876, on high ridges of the Siskiyou Mountains south of Waldo, Josephine County, Oregon. Lee's plant was published that year by Thomas C. Porter as *Calandrinia leana*, in honor of its discoverer. After a spell in the genus *Oreobroma*, it was placed in *Lewisia* (Robinson 1897). Although the epithet was originally given as "leana," an obvious misspelling of Lee's name, it appeared as "leeana" in Purdy's writing and elsewhere, and the latter spelling is now approved by most authorities, including W. T. Stearn, Brian Mathew, and Hershkovitz and Hogan.

A plant found by A. A. Heller on Mount Eddy in northern California was tentatively called *Oreobroma subalpinum* but never published; the Missouri Botanical Garden has proposed that it be regarded as a neotype of *Lewisia leeana*.

It is hard to understand how *Lewisia leeana* and *L. columbiana* could be

Lewisia leeana

confused, but they have been, at least in the literature. Their flowers are only superficially similar, and their foliage and inflorescences are quite distinct. The confusion originated in published misidentification of early herbarium material by the U.S. National Herbarium: the Columbia Gorge collections of *L. columbiana* by Louis F. Henderson and Thomas Jefferson Howell, as well as those by Sandberg and Leiberg from the Wenatchee Mountains, were taken to be *L. leeana*.

Purdy's *Lewisia eastwoodiana,* a white-flowered variant of *L. leeana,* was erroneously referred to *L. columbiana* (Elliott 1966). Specimens Purdy labeled *L. columbianum* and *L. columbianum roseum,* taken in the Siskiyous

A stunning combination of *Lewisia leeana* and *Phlox diffusa* at Kangaroo Lake in the Siskiyous VEVA STANSELL

in the 1930s, are in the herbarium of the California Academy of Sciences, and the plants offered in his catalogs were undoubtedly from there as well. Thus many misnamed lewisias got into gardens and were perpetuated under erroneous names.

Another source of confusion was the citation of *Lewisia columbiana* by Ferlatte (1974), who in his flora misidentified *L. ×whiteae*, a natural hybrid of *L. leeana* and *L. cotyledon*, which is occasional throughout the Klamath ranges. (This hybrid keys out nicely to *L. columbiana*!) Important floras have perpetuated the myth that *L. columbiana* is to be found in California, among them Hitchcock (1964) and Dempster (1993). Until it is well understood that *L. columbiana* is to be found only north of the Rogue River and *L. leeana* only south of it, the error will persist. Hohn (1975) determined that within section *Cotyledon*, these two species, though certainly lookalikes, are only remotely related.

Lewisia leeana is set apart from all others of its genus by its unique quill-shaped leaves, which persist through the year. Ira Gabrielson (1932) summed up its overall appearance: "It may be said to borrow the leaves of *Lewisia rediviva* and the numerous small flowers of *L. columbiana*."

These evergreen terete leaves can be as much as 3 inches (7.5 cm) long but are usually only about half that. They are borne atop the stalk in the typical concentric manner of a shaggy rosulate plant. In cross-section each leaf is round to oval; a few are quadrangular, suggesting the upper-and-lower surfaces common to all other lewisias except the bitter-

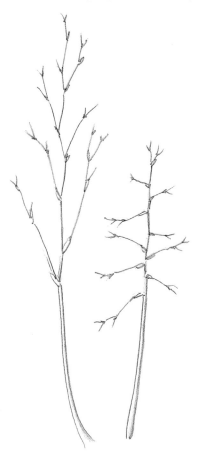

Lewisia columbiana (left) and *L. leeana*

roots. The leaves are acid green or covered with powdery glaucous bloom, in the latter case looking something like a succulent *Senecio* or an unflowered *Sedum*. It is not unusual for *Lewisia leeana* to assume the guise of a compact little ming tree with several erect branches to the caudex, each with its rosette of leaves. These narrow leaves may help the plant endure the bright sun, for it is commonly found where shade is nonexistent, as on the summit barrens of serpentine formations.

Although the flowers of *Lewisia leeana* are small compared to such species as *L. tweedyi* or *L. rediviva*, their numbers impart a very charming effect; someone once counted 377 flowers on a single plant. These are colored in a range from dark magenta-purple to lilac to white. Sometimes the color is concentrated in the petal tips to give a delicate spotted effect,

A charming specimen of *Lewisia leeana*, Castle Lake, Siskiyou County, California
MARGARET WILLIAMS

but usually the pigment is more evenly dispersed than in the veined or striped lewisias. An occasional white-flowered individual can be found in colored populations.

This unique species is found in all the ranges of the Klamath-Siskiyou region. Its northernmost known station is in the Rogue River drainage in Josephine County, Oregon. It ranges south to the Yolla Bolly Mountains in the Coast Range of northwestern Tehama County, California, growing at elevations from 4500 to 7500 feet (1370 to 2285 meters). It has also been known since approximately 1926 from a remarkably disjunct site some 300 miles (480 km) farther south in the Sierra Nevada in Fresno County. It is commonly confined to montane scree habitats or glacial

The white-flowered variant of *Lewisia leeana* (originally *L. eastwoodiana*) is found only in a few locations in the Siskiyous BURL MOSTUL

basins; its southernmost locality lies between 9000 and 10,000 feet (2745 and 3050 meters) in such a basin under open coniferous forest.

The plant Carl Purdy introduced in 1932 as *Lewisia eastwoodiana* (for Alice Eastwood) was originally brought to his nursery by one of his collectors, Mary White, who found it on cliffs of the Illinois Basin in Josephine County, Oregon. It had small white flowers with petals 6 to 8 mm long, borne in slender cymes 6 to 9 inches (15 to 23 cm) in length, each with two or three dozen flowers. The leaves, according to Purdy's description of it as it grew at his nursery in Ukiah, were a distinctive acid green.

Sampson Clay (1937) accurately noted that this plant was rather like *Lewisia leeana* in leaf and habit, with flowers in the color range of *L. columbiana* but held in tighter sprays. Since that time it has been erroneously referred to *L. columbiana*. Clay was obviously dealing with open-pollinated seedlings, as Purdy never described it as anything but white. Lester Rowntree compared its effect, as she observed it at Purdy's nursery, to that of white lace.

Examination of Purdy's type specimen at the California Academy of Sciences herbarium shows foliage quite typical for *Lewisia leeana* with its crowded stalk and square-angled branching arrangement. In the course of fieldwork on the evergreen species of section *Cotyledon*, Janet Hohn discovered, on a serpentine mountainside, an entire colony of exclusively white-flowered *L. leeana*, in the Klamath River drainage of Siskiyou County. The flowers, pollen, and seeds were all much larger than usual for the species. Exposed to intense light on this serpentine outcrop, the foliage here had a very glaucous quality, apparently the only significant difference between it and the Purdy type. This variant has recently been established in cultivation from seed gathered at the site.

Lewisia leeana is recorded as having been grown abroad as early as 1903 by A. K. Bulley of Bees' Seeds in England. Apparently outdone by the splendor of other exhibited lewisias, it has not won any RHS honors; however, one of its natural hybrids (with *L. cotyledon*), *L. ×whiteae* 'Margaret Williams', received an Award of Merit in 1967.

Lewisia serrata
L. R. Heckard & G. L. Stebbins 1974

Lewisia serrata is discussed with *Lewisia cantelovii,* beginning on page 55.

Section *Erocallis*

The section *Erocallis,* based on the monotypic genus *Erocallis* (Rydberg 1906), was erected by Mathew (1989). Some systematic botanists insist that its sole member, *Lewisia triphylla,* is not properly a member of *Lewisia,* yet they also insist that neither does it belong to *Claytonia:* they would prefer to retain Rydberg's interpretation. Australian botanist Roger Carolin (1987) believes that it clearly constitutes an intermediate genus, much as *L. tweedyi* does. Hershkovitz and Hogan plan to retain *L. triphylla* in *Lewisia.*

Lewisia triphylla
(S. Watson) B. L. Robinson 1897

Lewisia triphylla was, surprisingly, the very first species of *Lewisia* to be collected from the wild. According to the records of the Lewis and Clark expedition, it was discovered on 27 June 1806, four days before Lewis collected *Lewisia rediviva.* Lewis had found some tiny, precocious flowers among the snowbanks at the headwaters of the Kooskooskee (or Clearwater) River near Lolo Pass, and these could only have been *L. triphylla.* Perhaps because of the plants' fragility, these specimens did not reach Pursh, if indeed a collection was made, and the species was not found again until Sereno Watson collected it on California's Yuba River, above Camp Yuba (now Cisco), California, in 1867; he published it as *Claytonia triphylla* (Watson 1875).

    Lewisia triphylla became one of the components of the genus *Oreobroma* (Howell 1893) and was transferred with other members of that group to *Lewisia* (Robinson 1897). Per A. Rydberg (1906) removed it into

Lewisia triphylla

its own monotypic genus, *Erocallis*, but this proposal has not been widely accepted in recent years. (Colorado botanist William A. Weber, however, staunchly defended the opinions of Rydberg and such contemporaries of his as E. L. Greene.)

The plant explorer who digs up a little dormant portulacad tuber in this species's range has no way of knowing whether it is *Lewisia triphylla* or a *Claytonia*. Those familiar with the seedlings of both say that the leaves are linear in the *Lewisia* but broader in *Claytonia*—not very conclusive. The rootstock of this species is unique in the genus *Lewisia*: a tiny, almost spherical to ovoid tuber bearing on its lower surface scattered, hairlike roots, with a few frail leaves emerging from the upper surface, along with a very slender flowering stalk. The rootstock has also been referred to as a corm; Sampson Clay (1937) deftly avoided controversy by calling it a "little round earth nut," a common reference for geophytic food plants in the Old World. Tubers of *L. triphylla* were eaten by the native peoples of the American West.

Lewisia triphylla near Cisco, California MARGARET WILLIAMS

The basal leaves of *Lewisia triphylla* become dormant by flowering time, when the plant devotes its strength to reproduction. The whorl of stem leaves beneath the flower gives them the appearance of mingling with green leafy ribbons. The white to palest pink flowers are usually few, but on a flourishing plant a stem may bear as many as a dozen, with three or more stems per plant, all rising 2 to 3 inches (5 to 7.5 cm) above the ground. These flowers present quite a charming picture, as Marcel LePiniec once described them, in patches bordering tiny snowmelt rivulets in a mossy alpine meadow, their effect doubled, reflected in the quiet water.

In its habitat preferences, *Lewisia triphylla* seems close to the species of section *Pygmaea*, and it is commonly found growing with one or more of those. It is widely distributed: it reaches just into British Columbia, including Vancouver Island; it is found southward through the Cascade Range (but is absent from the Olympic Mountains), into the Klamath and California's North Coast Ranges, the Sierra Nevada, and the Warner Mountains. To the east it occurs in the northern Rocky Mountains from southernmost Alberta southward as far as northwestern Wyoming, Utah, and Colorado. Populations are also found in the Blue Mountains of Oregon and Washington, but it is nearly absent from the Great Basin ranges. Its sites are typical snowbank communities, as described in Chapter Two.

This is the kind of plant that delights the miniaturist, yet there are few reports of success in cultivation. It is a plant one may see often in the wild without focusing on its exquisite, millefleurs beauty. If it were two or three times as large and easily grown it would be a sensation, for examination with a hand lens shows it to be quite charming—perhaps the most precisely formed blossom in the genus.

Section *Lewisia*

Compact plants with stout, food-storing rootstocks, the three species in this section pass the hot, dry summer dormant below ground, recommencing growth in the cool days of autumn. Inhabitants of arid regions, they have "tumbleweed" inflorescences that disengage from the plant, stem and all, as the seed ripens; the dry stalk can be blown a considerable distance, dropping its seed along the way, especially in hospitable crevices where the capsule eventually lodges. The classification of this section and its members is generally agreed on, although one persistent botanist, Per A. Rydberg, insisted that these were the only true members of the genus *Lewisia*.

Lewisia disepala
P. A. Rydberg 1932

Lewisia disepala, also known as the alpine or Yosemite bitterroot, was found in 1891 by Mrs. Willie F. Dodd somewhere in Yosemite Valley. She brought the specimens to the California Academy of Sciences, where they and their records were destroyed in the San Francisco earthquake and fire of 1906. Mary Katharine Brandegee (1894) described it as *Lewisia rediviva* var. *yosemitana*. (Note: The same name was applied in 1912 by H. M. Hall to the plant now known as *L. kelloggii*.) Per A. Rydberg (1932) decided to elevate Brandegee's *L. rediviva* var. *yosemitana* to specific rank, but he could not follow the normal procedure of using the varietal epithet *yosemitana* for the species because in 1923 W. L. Jepson had designated Hall's plant *L. yosemitana*. In evident panic, Rydberg settled on the distinctly unuseful name of *L. disepala*, calling attention in the specific epithet to what was possibly the plant's most nonspecific characteristic: like almost all other lewisias, this species has only two sepals.

Lewisia disepala has a very restricted occurrence, limited principally to the granitic screes on and around the massive domes and cliffs in the vicinity of Yosemite National Park in the Sierra Nevada of California. Hikers in early spring—usually May at elevations above 6500 feet (1980 meters) in the Merced and Tuolumne river drainages—are likely to encounter snowbanks. Near the melting margins they may find the clumps of typical—but smaller—*L. disepala* foliage described so well by John

Lewisia disepala

Thomas Howell for volume 26 of the Sierra Club's *Bulletin* (as quoted in Elliott 1966, 31): "Queer little worm-like leaves formed a ragged collar about the beautiful rose-pink flowers which grew close to the ground and were about a half-inch across."

Like other lewisias, *Lewisia disepala* commences leaf growth in the cool of fall and passes the winter safe under the snow, shunning all exposures where the snow may be blown away. With the onset of spring warmth it is ready to flower, at a time when its frequent companion *L. kelloggii* is barely stirring.

The tint of the flowers ranges from very pale pink, near white, to soft amethyst and fuchsia. They are pearly miniatures of *Lewisia rediviva*, with each small blossom peeking from its brace of overbearingly large sepals. When the seeds have ripened, the stem falls away and the sepals become sails, catching the breezes that propel the entire dried inflorescence over the slopes, or even—in a remarkable feat of aerodynamics—across canyons to nearby scree ridges on updrafts.

The pearly *Lewisia disepala* SEAN HOGAN

This very charming miniature, once it has been introduced and properly understood, should become a favorite of alpine plant growers. Old plants can develop many crowns per caudex, each with multiple buds, and in flower the effect at a distance is reminiscent of precocious crocuses. Judging from the density of plants in wild colonies, seedlings develop quite fast; however, they can be extinguished just as fast if conditions are not ideal: they simply burn out when moisture fails. Unfortunately, *Lewisia disepala* has balked at cultivation, sometimes growing well but failing to open its buds. Brilliant light without heat is a requirement for flowering, and, of course, management of moisture levels is also critical to success.

Lewisia maguirei
A. H. Holmgren 1954

Sometimes, in an isolated backwater, a plant population appears that differs significantly from the more widespread species from which it seems to have developed. Genetic change may proceed to such an extent that the isolated plant is eventually defined by botanists as a distinct species or subspecies. Such singular populations, restricted to a small locality and unable to extend their range, may be thought of as "failed" species, having arisen at the wrong place or at the wrong time. Many are now candidates for endangered status, even though they are endangered chiefly by their own lack of fitness.

This process may be what occurred in the remote Quinn Canyon Range in Nevada's Great Basin, where on 8 July 1945 a pair of Utah botanists discovered plants obviously related to yet curiously unlike the familiar bitterroot. They did not publish their find until 1954, when one of them, Arthur Holmgren, described it and named it for his colleague, Bassett Maguire, who by that time had left Nevada for the New York Botanical Garden, where he held a position of some honor for many years.

We do not know precisely how rare *Lewisia maguirei* is, nor do we

Lewisia maguirei

clearly understand its position within the phylogeny of the genus. It is unlikely that it was ever widespread. In fact, Holmgren believed from the outset that it was restricted to the type locality, Cherry Creek Summit. Over the years it has been found occasionally one mile (1.5 km) to the east and, recently, 5 miles (8 km) to the west, in the headwaters of Sawmill Canyon, and to the north in the Grant Range—both range extensions of some significance, according to the indefatigable Jerry DeSanto of Montana (pers. comm. 1998). There may well be other sites in huge Nye County, Nevada, an area of more than 18,000 square miles (46,620 sq km) with a population of fewer than four thousand people—only a handful of whom are probably aware of the endemic lewisia.

Although *Lewisia maguirei* grows along with *L. rediviva*, the two are

Cherry Creek Summit, where *Lewisia maguirei* was discovered in 1945
JOHN MASSEY/PHILIP BAULK

easily distinguishable when in growth. The leaves of *L. maguirei* are linear-lanceolate and flat-bladed, with an obvious midrib, in contrast to the more terete leaves of the bitterroot. The flowers are also distinct: in *L. maguirei* they are not solitary but usually borne in short, lax cymes of two or three blossoms, with fewer, huskier, and more prominent bracts. Moreover, the flowers are smaller than those of *L. rediviva* and have fewer petals. Their color is always pallid, whitish to pinkish. The seven to nine large sepals function like those of other lewisias, helping to propel the disengaged individual capsules on the wind.

The Quinn Canyon Range is one of many blocky mountain ridges that partition the Great Basin into about ninety smaller subbasins. *Lewisia maguirei* grows at elevations of 7500 to 8500 feet (2285 to 2590 meters), close enough to Troy Peak (11,268 feet; 3435 meters) that its habitat is undoubtedly modified by the precipitation caught there, much of it as snow.

The rare *Lewisia maguirei*, growing on a limestone slope in an isolated area of southeastern Nevada BURL MOSTUL

Visitors unfamiliar with the high desert are always surprised to find how many sparkling streams flow off these ranges as the snows melt, supporting a wealth of wildflowers and of birds; but the streams are going nowhere fast and soon disappear into the thirsty atmosphere or sink into the basin floor, a few dying as playas in the broad flatness.

The exposed limestone slopes where *Lewisia maguirei* grows appear devoid of small understory plants except in very early spring. Where some shelter and weathering permit the accumulation of a gummy soil, a pine or juniper accents the scrub cover, which shelters bulbs, phloxes, and a few other showy flowers. The limestone has weathered to lovely soft, subtle colors and gentle contours, with conifers marking the upper snow zone and shad-scrub the lower zone, down near the flatland. On the cooler north slope *L. maguirei* grows under a continuous but light conifer cover in gravelly clearings.

When describing such a rare plant, I am reminded of a story. Two venerable gentlemen meet year after year, unplanned but regularly, in a remote wild place; they acknowledge each other with only a nod and quickly move on. After many such meetings, one fellow finally ventured to ask the reason for the other's visits; he received this reply: "I have heard that the rarest and most beautiful of flowers grows here, and I hope to find it myself. And you?"

"Yes," the first man said, "I too know of this rare and beautiful flower; and I come to pick off all its buds so no one else will find it!"

The lack of proliferation seen in *Lewisia maguirei*, however, is surely natural. In view of its narrow endemism, *L. maguirei* was proposed in June 1979 to be listed in the Federal Register of Endangered Species; it has not been listed as of this writing, but the Nevada Natural Heritage Program recognizes the plant as a "sensitive species," one that is "critically imperiled." For the time being, it is holding its own against great environmental stress. The species has not proven easy to establish in cultivation, although Bob Putnam once offered nursery-grown plants.

Lewisia rediviva
F. T. Pursh 1814

Lewisia rediviva attracted more interest than any other plant brought back by the Lewis and Clark expedition for its dried specimen's sideshow ability to return to life. Later collectors were eager to find and introduce it, not just as a curiosity but as a potential food plant: Edward Palmer (1871) wrote a report for the U.S. Department of Agriculture on its possibilities as a cultivated food crop. In 1838 Asa Gray reported that Thomas Nuttall in Philadelphia had received herbarium material from Nathaniel Wyeth; this was sent to Joseph Dalton Hooker at Kew. (Wyeth reportedly received the plant from John McCloud, who had collected the plant near a fur trapper's summer rendezvous on Wyoming's Green River in 1837.) Hooker, upon examining its dried buds, satisfied himself that *Lewisia rediviva* was indeed a portulacad and published a description elaborating on that of Pursh (1814). Gray also noted that the Horticultural Society (later the Royal Horticultural Society) had received specimens of the same plant from their great plant explorer, David Douglas.

Douglas's first shipments of North American plants arrived in England in 1826, but *Lewisia rediviva* was not among them. He did not encounter the bitterroot until May 1826, after he had traveled up the Columbia River from the coast with a Hudson Bay Company brigade. Douglas left his party at Fort Colville (in what is now northeastern Washington) to wander with his packhorses about the vast Columbia River Basin at his usual determined pace—one that would tire us today—from the Okanogan Highlands south to the Blue Mountains, and from the Cascade foothills east into present-day Idaho. He surveyed first for flowering specimens and later returned for seed, even if it meant covering the same ground a third time.

In March 1827, Douglas found lewisias growing in the gravels of upper Columbia River tributaries. He collected specimens and brought them in his baggage overland across Canada to the Hudson Bay and thence to England.

Lewisia rediviva var. *rediviva*

Despite all the effort, this attempt to introduce the bitterroot failed. The plants produced only vegetative growth for a short time in the garden of the RHS before they perished. Thus the plant did not flower in England until 1863, at the Royal Botanic Gardens, Kew, from material brought to Kew by David Lyall from southcentral British Columbia.

Lewisia rediviva belongs to the xeric element of the western American flora that seems to have moved northward as the postglacial climate became both warmer and drier. It occupies an arid habitat, cold in winter and dry in summer, yet not as parched as a true desert. Although almost all lewisias are considered xeric plants, the bitterroot is the one most nearly suited to the desert; perhaps it evolved in the warm Southwest before that region had become so dry and hot. The true deserts of the West now exist almost exclusively in the rain shadows of the Sierra Nevada and other ranges. The bitterroot, however, is only occasional in the northerly, semidesert extensions of this zone, as it is found in some shortgrass prairies and in the so-called cold desert or sagebrush steppe.

Lewisia rediviva is distributed widely throughout the West, mainly in the intermountain region but also outside it. Of the genus, only *L. pygmaea* has a wider range. In southern California it is known to frequent high, dry, serpentine-derived soils within view of the Pacific Ocean in the Santa Monica Mountains; it also occurs not far above sea level on the Diablo Range near San Francisco Bay. East of the Rocky Mountains it extends into favorable sites, with its extreme northeastern colonies on the Great Plains in Wyoming near the border of South Dakota. The characteristic common to these widely dispersed habitats is a dry climate without heavy rainfall at any

A fine, deep rose-colored *Lewisia rediviva* var. *rediviva* growing on serpentine soils, Lake County, California MARGARET WILLIAMS

time, and a long cool growing season. The bitterroot is best adapted where much of the annual precipitation falls as snow, and few populations are established in sites not subject to consistently cold temperatures in mid-winter.

The species has extended its range across the Continental Divide of the northern Rockies. In Montana it has not progressed far beyond the eastern slopes of the Rockies, but in Wyoming it has been aggressively successful around South Pass, a 30-mile (48-km) long plateau at approximately 7550 feet (2500 meters) elevation. East of South Pass, impelled no doubt by the prevailing westerly winds, it has spread as far as the Laramie Plains in southeastern Wyoming, 180 miles (290 km) beyond that pass with a few southward dashes into northernmost Colorado.

Lewisia rediviva var. *rediviva* by the acre, spaced in cold desert fashion, Craters of the Moon, Idaho TOM KNIGHT

Claude Barr (1983) wrote that *Lewisia rediviva* in its most easterly advance had "slipped away from the paternal roof of the Big Horn Mountains to spread a wide salient on the Great Plains"; he foresaw the day when "a whirling air current will waft a cargo of seeds across the narrow Belle Fourche valley . . . the final forty miles of Wyoming will be entered"—and the bitterroot will have reached the Dakotas.

Some writers have suggested that the bitterroot's outlying populations resulted from deliberate introduction by native peoples who used it as a food, but there is no oral or written record of its having been cultivated. A recent report of its occurrence in Alberta along the Old North Trail of the Blackfoot people is interesting, but this population appears to fit the usual pattern for all the genus—locally abundant and with broad discontinuities separating colonies. (Nevertheless, it is interesting that this is one of the very few Canadian records not in the Columbia River drainage, lying as it does in the headwaters of the Saskatchewan River, which drains

Another Lake County, California, bitterroot, this one with an attractive white eye SEAN HOGAN

northeasterly to Hudson Bay.) Such discontinuities can be explained by natural phenomena. Migrations along the valleys and ridges of north-south mountain chains have left straggling remnant populations of many *Lewisia* species widely isolated, scattered hither and yon.

The preferred substrates of *Lewisia rediviva* are usually gritty or stony and well drained, but in the driest regions it tolerates dense clay soils that are seldom really wet. It also does well in the snowbed habitat, where it may even be inundated in spring. Perhaps because its real need is for a lack of competition, the bitterroot can prosper as well in near-desert steppe as in the snowbeds above it, as long as it can enjoy a dry-summer resting period.

Although limestone soils often support bitterroot, it does not seem to require alkalinity to thrive. In much of California, particularly in the Coast Range, it flourishes on serpentine and other ultrabasic formations. It is remarkable to walk out on a stark serpentine barren abloom with these sumptuous blossoms in the glare of the April sun, to find flowers that seem to have sprung from nothing at all, with almost no plant companions for relief. Among the few plants that tolerate the toxic minerals of such barrens are the oak *Quercus durata* and the xeric fern *Aspidotis densa;* species of *Cryptanthus* and the brilliant purple *Allium falcifolium* flower along with the bitterroot.

Bitterroot plants usually grow where they receive full sun, although some individuals are to be found in slightly shaded niches. Close to the ground, *Lewisia rediviva* is surrounded by a great sweep of open space; by contrast, its evergreen relatives seem like chained captives on their cliffs and canyon walls.

The annual growth of *Lewisia rediviva* commences almost imperceptibly in the cool of fall, about the time of the first frost in most cases, without any apparent need for triggering by rainfall or daylength. Growth continues through winter, snowbound or exposed, even in freezing conditions, until about the time of the last spring frost, at which time the flower buds are well developed. During its active period the plant withstands both soggy, saturated soils and freezing cold without damage, since its root system is in strong growth.

A mature crown has about two dozen plump leaves like tiny green fingers. Among them appear the large, spindle-shaped flower buds, from a few to eight or ten per crown on a vigorous plant, each on its own short stalk. As the buds rise, the leaves, seemingly exhausted by the effort, begin to collapse "in wisps of dead string," as Reginald Farrer put it (to which another frustrated garden writer added, "And hope is dying with them"). Like the spongy leaves of many other succulent plants, they become not only thinner but also shorter as they dry up; this shrinkage in herbarium material has contributed to much uncertainty and many misleading and even erroneous descriptions. It is interesting that among populations, or even within a single population, the leaves of some plants persist much longer than others. Different plants also seem to have varying resistance to rust infection and to predation by mice (Daubenmire 1975).

Some degree of chilling—greater than the cooling needed for fall leaf formation—is necessary to initiate flower buds; plants grown in heated greenhouses do not flower (Daubenmire 1975). In addition, leaves on greenhouse plants tended to be erect, rather than prostrate as in the wild.

The exposed buds, plump with dark promise, lie there stubbornly as the sun rises higher and the land dries. Then, one clement morning, the first bud raises itself to open "into the most improbable flower ever to appear on the desert landscape, rivaling the splendor of any cactus in bloom" (Gabrielson 1932). The blossoms have often been compared to those of waxen water lilies, but they are really more like silky cactus flowers.

The continued opening of the flowers appears to be controlled not by sunlight but by warmth during the middle part of the day. Rex Daubenmire (1975) experimented with excluding insect pollinators and found that some unfertilized flowers continued to open for up to six days, though most balked at more than two. This suggests that a strain with an extended flowering period might be selected for cultivation.

After the blossom has been fertilized by insects, it fades but sheds none of its parts except for the pollen. The withering petals and stamens fold inward to wrap the ovary in a tidy package bound within the six to nine sepals. The seed takes only a short time to ripen, and then the plant's real genius emerges. The stalk disengages at the point marked by the whorl of bracts, and the papery calyx and its enclosed capsule cartwheel away along the surface or are lifted high on the little whirlwinds common to these arid lands in early summer. The last blossoms may still be opening as the first capsules are whisked away.

These seed vessels eventually come to rest against some natural barrier, such as a rocky ledge, or in a lee hollow. In such sites humus and wind-blown soil also accumulate, and snow is likely to drift in, providing a fully furnished seedbed. During the journey, or at its end, the capsule splits around near its base and pops its top, revealing the shiny black, disk-shaped seeds, which adhere in a little clutch for a while. Their release completes the bitterroot's life story.

The short, thick caudex of a bitterroot plant may remain single, or it may develop multiple crowns. In his remarkable study, Daubenmire (1975) cited one individual with thirty-eight crowns, so crowded that no flowers were produced. Plants that have become exposed by wind erosion may develop adventitious crowns from the sides of the caudices. The root system of the bitterroot, like those of many of its companion plants, is very shallow; most of the hair roots of such plants are of only annual duration. The caudex can survive desiccation during hot summer days as long as those are balanced by cool nights.

Lewisia rediviva is well adapted to survival in sites where natural processes resculpt the surface. When Mount Saint Helens in southern Washington erupted in May 1980, the bitterroots to the east, in fat bud stage, were buried by up to 2 inches (5 cm) of volcanic ash or tephra. Many of the plants were able to punch through this cementlike coat, open their flowers, and produce seed. In certain places along the Columbia River, such as near Vantage, the fine tuff still tops the pillow basalt, smothering lichens and mosses, but the bitterroots are undiminished; in fact, this deposit appears to act as a beneficial barrier mulch, conserving moisture. Sometimes soft plants such as lewisias must remain dormant through several seasons because they are incapable of muscling through this sort of barrier. In other instances, bitterroots buried in mudflows have pushed up through one inch (2.5 cm) or more of compacted clay, baked into a hard surface barrier.

Only in dimension does *Lewisia rediviva* var. *minor*, the miniature bitterroot, differ from the typical "Montana" bitterroot. The precedent for the name comes from Rydberg's *L. minor*, a legitimate name though not necessarily a sound taxon; Philip A. Munz (1959) demoted *L. minor* to a variety of *L. rediviva*. Arthur Holmgren (1954) expanded the taxon to subspecies rank. It seems, however, to be only a weak phase of this widespread species, probably the result of environmental stress and not a genetic variety. Brian Mathew (1989) allowed that the "diminutive variant"

of *L. rediviva* may be recognized as subspecies *minor*. Hogan and Hershkovitz plan to revert to Munz's account of *L. rediviva* var. *minor* and to restrict its range from Oregon to the southern Sierra Nevada and Tooele County, Utah. A transplantation study would shed some light on the matter.

The range of *Lewisia rediviva* var. *minor* is considered to be rocky, flat areas (whether flats or higher areas such as mesas and ridges) at elevations from 6500 to 9000 feet (1980 to 2745 meters) in the Sierran rain shadow, which nonetheless experiences a good deal of moisture in spring due to poor drainage. Companion plants are typically sagebrush, juniper, piñon, and yellow pines. The flowers of the smaller bitterroot are

March brings a sturdy line-up of *Lewisia rediviva* var. *minor*, Black Hills, Lake County, Oregon SEAN HOGAN

commonly white to ivory, but pink flowers are found as well. It seems to occur with the larger type.

In recent drought years in the northern extension of the Great Basin in Oregon, in the vicinity of Christmas Valley and the Albert Rim of Lake County, unusually small bitterroots have been found, yet they have flowered and seeded. Their habitat is an area of lava formations and pluvial lake basins. A good part of the moisture in this area comes as a fine powder snow that collects thinly in the lees, and just blows around until it drops out of sight. The number of flowers in such "snowbeds" is surprising for all the harshness of the habitat. In these circumstances, plants are surely very old, and the mortality rate of seedlings must be very high.

Pursh (1814) originally described *Lewisia rediviva*'s flowers as being white, and white-flowered bitterroot is not uncommon, either in pure stands or as occasional plants in otherwise pink-flowered populations. The white variants are least common in the northern Rocky Mountains. Sir Joseph Dalton Hooker mentioned *L. rediviva flore-alba* in 1860, and

A white-flowered *Lewisia rediviva* var. *rediviva* blooms in April on Mount Diablo, near San Francisco Bay, California SEAN HOGAN

Albert Kellogg described and illustrated *L. alba* but did not cite a specimen or locality; neither is presently recognized as a valid taxon.

White or ivory flowers must rely on perfection of form and finish to compete in popularity with colored forms, and the white bitterroot (and other white lewisias) are among the most exquisite of wildflowers. The white bitterroot is never more striking than when seen in the glinting light of the lava fields of southern Idaho's Craters of the Moon. Early in the day, before the dew has evaporated from these broad plains, their closed flowers are almost invisible among the white-felted tuffets of *Eriogonum ovalifolium* dotted across the broad plain of dark cinder. As the morning warms, a magical transformation occurs: the silken white lewisias open silently and magically among these flannel ghosts, with the tiny bright purple annual *Mimulus nanus* filling the spaces between.

Growers both in America and abroad have from time to time selected choice forms of *Lewisia rediviva* from among their seedlings. Kath Dryden in England has received many awards for lewisias exhibited in British shows, but she is to be especially commended for developing the Jolon (pronounced ho-LONE) Strain of *L. rediviva*. The original clone 'Jolon' received the Royal Horticultural Society's Award of Merit in 1976; as exhibited, 'Jolon' bore five open ivory-pink flowers and several more buds—no mean accomplishment in southern England with a plant better suited to the Iberian Peninsula. The clone came from seed collected around 1970 by the great California plantsman Wayne Roderick near the historic Mission San Antonio de Padua at Jolon, Monterey County, California, where the scattered plants grew in a thin soil of oak humus and grass fiber over the stones of an old streambed. This colony has since been largely destroyed by highway development. The broad-petaled flowers open to 3 inches (7.5 cm) wide, and the leaves are long for the species. It is said to be easier in cultivation than most bitterroots. Color strains, such as the Champagne Strain, have now been introduced.

Less famous is a strain known in the Pacific Northwest as *Lewisia rediviva* 'Teanaway Rose', which was selected from a population of plants

growing in Washington's central Cascades in the drainage of the Teanaway River, Kittitas County. Here the bitterroot dwells not in the valleys but
on rocky summits up to 4000 feet (1220 meters) elevation, where it receives the needed sun. The flowers are a soft, muted old rose shade, varying to pale blush; they are broad-petaled and up to 3 inches (7.5 cm) wide.
This strain has been grown well at the Göteborg Botanical Garden in Swe-
den and other European gardens.

A "yellow" bitterroot known to gardeners as "Watson's phase" has been
found in the wild as a few individuals growing among a colony of white-
and rose-flowered plants in Montana's Bitterroot Valley. Henry Grant,
whose garden there was famous for its bitterroot display, did not consider
it very yellow. A photograph on page 55 of *Bitterroot* (DeSanto 1993)
shows a cold white flower with yellow anthers and filaments within a calyx
of green sepals, with no hint of the rosy suffusion common to the species;
in this respect it bears some similarity to *Lewisia maguirei*. DeSanto iden-
tifies these plants with an individual described by Sereno Watson (1871).
The Montana plant is in limited cultivation from seed. It appears more
nearly yellow than other white-petaled lewisias; the tint may best be described as old ivory. It should be noted that "yellow-flowered" plants have

appeared among hybrids between *L.
rediviva* and other species. Isolated ex-
amples of yellow flowers have been observed in *L. disepala* and *L. maguirei* as
well (DeSanto 1998).

Lewisia rediviva 'Winifred Herdman'
received the RHS Award of Merit when
exhibited by C. van Tubergen in 1927,
but this strain, reported as "having large
flowers of an almost purple hue," has
apparently vanished from cultivation in
Britain (Elliott 1966). Sampson Clay
(1937) pronounced this selection "ro-

Lewisia rediviva 'Teanaway Rose'
TOM KNIGHT

buster and rather easier to manage than the finicky type." Perhaps its descendants survive in some Victoria gardens. The name commemorates Winifred Barnes (née Herdman), wife of nurseryman Hyland Barnes, of Vancouver and later Victoria, British Columbia; they are believed to have gathered the seed from which the strain originated during holiday visits to the dry belt of central British Columbia. Deep color has also been noted in bitterroots in the province's Kootenai Valley, where the lewisia population was largely drowned by Lake Koocanusa behind a hydroelectric dam.

Section *Pygmaea*

The section *Pygmaea* proposed by Brian Mathew (1989) was based on the informal "*Pygmaea* group" of Roy Elliott (1966). Even earlier, this natural alliance was known to such veteran growers as John Heckner and Carl Purdy, who mentioned it in their nursery catalogs in the 1930s.

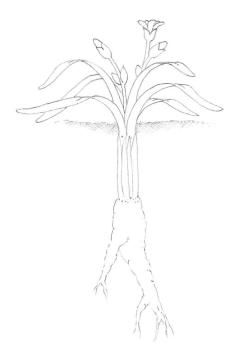

Mathew's scheme is here altered to encompass two other sections of his, treating these as three clusters: *Brachycalyx*, *Oppositifolia*, and *Pygmaea*. Thus my proposed section *Pygmaea* brings together all lewisias in which an annual growth of foliage and flowers emerge together in spring from a fascicle of growth from the deep-seated rootstock, contained within a tube of tissue that assists the emergence but does not itself appear above ground.

In contrast to the other deciduous lewisias, the species of section *Pygmaea* show no sign of growth until the warmth and moisture of spring arrive. At higher eleva-

Section *Pygmaea*: emergence, showing pre-emergent sheath

tions this may not occur until July; lower-elevation plants by that time may already have retreated below ground into summer dormancy.

The species of section *Pygmaea* occupy lofty, cool places. They are widespread: in the north they extend to eastern Alaska, the unglaciated Yukon Valley and its basin in Canada, the Saint Elias region of southeastern Alaska and northern British Columbia, and southeast barely to the mountains of Alberta; in the south, they are found in the Rio Grande Basin of New Mexico and the southern extremes of the western American cordillera westward in Arizona, southern California, and Baja California. Between these extremes they have taken suitable habitations throughout the West.

These plants experience really moist soil only in the snowmelt season, when they are emerging. At this time of rapid growth they appreciate and even demand quantities of moving water, surviving even the occasional submergence without damage. As they later prepare to pass the short dry summer in relatively cool places, these small plants drain the last of their strength from the shriveling foliage to aid in ripening their copious seed.

As considered here, section *Pygmaea* has three clusters and eight species. The many published names that have been applied to these taxa bear witness to their great variability.

Brachycalyx Cluster

The many similarities of *Lewisia brachycalyx* and *L. kelloggii* would tempt a conservative herbarium botanist to consider them members of a single species—a pair of subspecies allied by the similar characteristics that also isolate them from all other species of *Lewisia*. Indeed, Sereno Watson placed John Muir's early collection of *L. kelloggii* in *L. brachycalyx*. More than other lewisias, these two species bear the nearest general resemblance to their Central and South American cousins, the stemless *Calandrinia* species.

The two may be distinguished by several traits. *Lewisia brachycalyx*

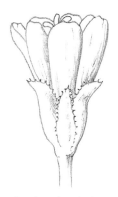

Brachycalyx cluster: bracts and sepals

forms a rosette 4 to 6 inches (10 to 15 cm) in diameter, with distinctly lanceolate leaves and sepals with entire margins; it ranges from central Arizona and extreme southwestern Utah to southern California and northernmost Baja California, Mexico. *Lewisia kelloggii* has a smaller and less formal rosette 2 to 3 inches (5 to 7.5 cm) across, ovate leaves with indented or retrorse apex, and glandular-toothed sepals; it is found in the north-central Sierra Nevada, with a disjunct population on the central Idaho granitic batholith. Although these two species bear little semblance to each other, for the purposes of classification they are juxtaposed here.

Lewisia brachycalyx
G. Engelmann ex A. Gray 1868

"It is no easy matter to find suitable words, nor to coin adequate phrases to portray such ethereal beauty, ineffable purity and gleaming loveliness in blossoms at once translucent, ice-white and crystalline," wrote W. H. N. Preece (1937), trying to fix *Lewisia brachycalyx* on the page. "A will-o'-the-wisp in the marshes of memory with a softness of texture hardly to be associated with ice-white or crystalline," he further ventured, before settling on the perfect comparison, "white jade."

This species was first described in 1868, as *Calandrinia brachycalyx*, by George Engelmann from specimens collected in southwestern Utah (in May 1857 by William H. Brewer in the Great Basin), in western New Mexico (by John Newberry), and in Arizona (in 1865 by Elliott Coues and Edward Palmer near Fort Whipple, now Prescott). The epithet refers to the short, broad calyx. Asa Gray renamed it *Lewisia brachycalyx* later that same year, noting that its habit was similar to that of *L. pygmaea* and *C. acaulis*, but also that it was "necessarily associated with *Lewisia* on ac-

Lewisia brachycalyx

count of the number of petals and dehiscence of the capsule." He also mentioned its fragrance, a quality seldom found in this genus.

The populations presently found in the Southwest are undoubtedly small remnants of a once widely dispersed Madrian species in pre-Sierran times, before that interior region became so arid and eroded. Although initially reported from western New Mexico, *Lewisia brachycalyx* has never again been collected there; however, it is frequent in adjacent Arizona, occurring in great numbers in the uplands of Apache, Coconino, Gila, Navajo, and Yavapai counties on the mountain ridge of central Arizona, an ancient westward-extending spine of the Rockies. Large distances typically separate its colonies, especially the westernmost ones, with disjunct occurrences in southwestern Utah, in southern California, and in northern Baja California. There are colonies in the San Bernardino Mountains, with the westernmost locality near Lake Cuyamaca in San Diego County.

This southern lewisia can be found in a variety of habitats. All are parched but sheltered for half the year or more, well watered during the cool months, and soaked by snowmelt in the growing season. It has been reported on sandy lakeshores, in rock pavements, and on highly fossilized limestone gravels, usually under high shade of oaks, pines, or junipers, but also on open grassy slopes and swales.

Although it is one of the smaller lewisias, *Lewisia brachycalyx* is no miniature; in fact, its visual effect is rather bold. This species is a charmer in anybody's book. The handsome, usually simple rosette can reach 5 inches (12.5 cm) across but is usually only two-thirds that. It rises from a deeply plunging, stout rootstock. In bright sunlight these striking rosettes assume a ruddy cast, which may vary with the depth of pink coloration in the flowers. Entirely lacking pedicels, the flowers huddle over the foliage, sometimes so closely as to conceal all but the tips of the leaves. Each lovely goblet-shaped blossom is composed of five to nine petals, spreading 1.5 inches (3.5 cm), opening widely by day but closing at dusk.

However pretty, no two plants are exact duplicates. Betty Lowry wrote

The bluffs of the Salt River Canyon in Arizona are good habitat for *Lewisia brachycalyx* SEAN HOGAN in a letter that there are within *Lewisia brachycalyx* "leaves from narrow to pointed to those approaching spoon-shaped and blunt; the flowers, too, [vary] in both size and color, from white to clear pink, with pollen from creamy white to nearly black, those giving a smudged effect." The pink tones are variable; even on the same plant different flowers may be mottled, faintly striped, or clear, reverting to white in some seasons.

In its natural habitat this is a precocious plant, coming into both growth and flower early and soon entering its summer rest, or estivation. Where moisture continues to be available, it can be coaxed to continue producing both leaves and flowers, even while maturing its seeds. It may be possible to select a long-flowering strain in cultivation.

A charming specimen of *Lewisia brachycalyx*, just after seasonal snowmelt in Gila County, Arizona SEAN HOGAN

In the open garden *Lewisia brachycalyx* ought not to be any more difficult than *L. columbiana*, wedged among large rocks in a sand bed and fed occasionally (see the discussion in Chapter Six, "Lewisias in Containers"). Here it may behave just as in nature; with controlled watering, however, it may continue flowering for a surprisingly long period in a sheltered location. Its early emergence may necessitate the shelter of a pane of glass to keep rain and snow from damaging the new growth. The plant is hardy and will recover, but any plant in tatters is hardly a thing of beauty. Such protection against winter wet is also insurance against damage by freezing and consequent decay.

A small lewisia persisting under

the name *Lewisia brachycalyx* in the nursery trade of western Europe is an impostor—probably a form of *L. nevadensis*. The confusion probably arose in the 1920s or 1930s, when *L. brachycalyx* was described from several cool, moist sites in southern California. At about the same time, another lewisia from the same habitat was described, as *L. bernardina*; this plant was later submerged in *L. nevadensis*, and Sampson Clay (1937) dismissed it as "a smaller and inferior version of" *L. brachycalyx*. One wonders what plant he actually had before him: *L. brachycalyx* leaves could never be called needle-like. At some point, in any case, the two must have become confused in the trade. The plant grown under the name today may even be a highly fertile hybrid.

Lewisia kelloggii
M. K. Brandegee 1894

San Francisco physician and naturalist Albert C. Kellogg found his lewisia flowering in old glacial beds of granite sand in the central Sierra Nevada in late June 1870. He was traveling east from Sacramento with the botanist H. N. Bolander and other companions beyond the railroad construction site at Camp Yuba (now Cisco) on the Yuba River. The party followed the old Overland Emigrant Trail up to Donner Pass, finding this little unknown plant with *Lewisia nevadensis* and *L. triphylla* alongside the rutted wagon route near the summit. Since then both a railway and a highway (Interstate 80) have been built on this route, but there is still room for the lewisias.

Mary Katharine Brandegee (1894) described Kellogg's specimens in the course of her work with the California Academy of Sciences. Unfortunately, the type specimen was lost in the 1906 San Francisco earthquake and fire; W. L. Jepson's collection of July 1911 is regarded as the neotype. His field notes describe the plant as "just pushing forth from the sand atop El Capitan overlooking Yosemite Valley, with flowers right on the surface suggesting diamonds in the crown of this most eminent granite dome."

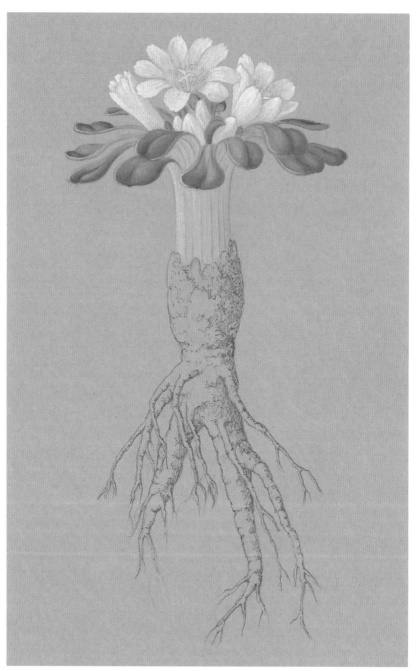

Lewisia kelloggii subsp. *kelloggii*

Other names have been applied to Kellogg's lewisia over the years. In 1912 H. M. Hall designated it *Lewisia rediviva* var. *yosemitana* (the plant Brandegee described by this name in 1894 is now considered to be *L. disepala*); in 1923 W. L. Jepson designated it *L. yosemitana*; and like other members of section *Pygmaea*, it was included for a time in Rydberg's genus *Oreobroma.*

Lewisia kelloggii displays certain obvious similarities to *L. brachycalyx.* Unlike *L. brachycalyx*, however, *L. kelloggii* has not developed a following among gardeners. Although it has flowered in research assemblages, it has never become securely established either in private collections or in commerce. Nonetheless, it is every bit as beautiful as its more popular cousin. This exquisite gem is nearly unknown even to wildflower enthusiasts, simply because they usually visit too late in the season to catch its flowering. It deserves better recognition in gardens and in the wild.

The bell-shaped flower of *Lewisia kelloggii*, which may be white, off-white, or pinkish lilac, is held erect, like a tiny tulip on a very short stalk. It is only about half the size of the bells of *L. brachycalyx*, which are held at an angle. Another feature distinguishing the two species is the margins of the sepals and bracts, which are smooth in *L. brachycalyx* and minutely glandular-toothed in *L. kelloggii.*

Lewisia kelloggii flowers along with or shortly after the spring snowmelt, from May to July depending on elevation. In a month or so the seed is maturing as the dry foliage stands erect and intact. Windblown granite dust and grit enshrouds these marcescent crowns like a mummy case, often before the seed is dispersed. Late in the season small rodents often dig the starchy roots for food, scattering the dry crowns with their cargo of seed; late flowers may be

Lewisia kelloggii subsp. *kelloggii* near Truckee, in the Sierra Nevada SEAN HOGAN

observed still opening in response to the warmth of the sun even after the rootstock has been consumed. This method of seed dispersal may partly explain why this species exists in only a few widely disjunct colonies but is locally plentiful at those sites.

The total range of *Lewisia kelloggii* extends more than 1000 miles (1600 km), from Madera County in California's central Sierra Nevada to central Idaho—with a 500-mile (800-km) gap between the California and Idaho populations. The region between has been devastated by recent and on-going volcanic activity, which has covered all the deep, cool granite sand deposits favored by this plant.

During the 1940s, C. Leo Hitchcock and J. W. Thompson speculated that *Lewisia kelloggii* appeared to be a very old species headed for extinction, and that its absence between the Sierra Buttes of Plumas County, California, and the Idaho batholith was so unusual that it just might occur somewhere in the intervening area but had simply been overlooked. Fifty years after this observation was published in *Leaflets of Western Botany*, however, *L. kelloggii* has still not been recorded in this gap, where the Cascade Range extends into California.

The California populations of *Lewisia kelloggii* grow between 4500 and 7700 feet (1370 and 2360 meters) elevation in the Sierra Nevada from Madera County north to Plumas County. The northern colonies feature both white and lilac flowers. Companion plants may include *Calyptridium* and other species of *Lewisia* (usually *L. nevadensis* or *L. triphylla*); *Allium* and *Eriogonum* species; *Artemisia arbuscula*, *Penstemon newberryi*, and occasionally *Calochortus luteus*. The Idaho populations do not appear to differ much from the California plants in spite of their centuries of isolation, with only creamy white flowers known. The latter colonies exist at higher elevations, up to 10,000 feet (3050 meters), and consequently flower later, up to mid-August. On the Idaho batholith in Custer, Elmore, Lemhi, and Valley counties, they are found in granite chippings from exfoliating cliffs near melting snow.

Much larger than the type in all respects, *Lewisia kelloggii* subsp. *hutch-*

isonii, found in 1982 on Saddleback Mountain in Sierra County, California, by Lauramay Dempster and Paul Hutchison, is exclusively pink-flowered (Dempster 1996).

Oppositifolia Cluster

Two species from the northern Coast and Klamath ranges of California and adjacent Oregon have certain similarities, yet they are distinct enough that they are not likely to be confused. Both are endemic to ultrabasic substrates or serpentines, and both form irregular rosettes with a few multiflowered stems. *Lewisia oppositifolia*, found only in Del Norte County, California, and adjacent Josephine County, Oregon, has an erect inflorescence of white flowers; *L. stebbinsii*, from Mendocino, Trinity, and Tehama counties of California, has a decumbent inflorescence of rose-mauve flowers with a faded pink or white eye.

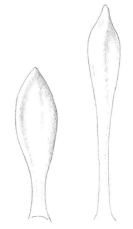

Oppositifolia cluster: leaves of *Lewisia stebbinsii* (left) and *L. oppositifolia*

Lewisia oppositifolia
(S. Watson) B. L. Robinson 1897

Lewisia oppositifolia was first collected by Thomas Jefferson Howell in 1883 in Josephine County, Oregon; the specimen was sent to Harvard University, where Sereno Watson described it in 1885 as *Calandrinia oppositifolia*; Howell (1893) incorporated it into his new genus *Oreobroma*, and Robinson (1897) brought it into *Lewisia*. Like so many other western plants, its discovery was linked to the gold fields, which were readily accessible to exploring naturalists.

The gold camp in this case, high in the Siskiyou Mountains, was Waldo, which also served as the base camp for the surveying party that fixed the border between California and Oregon; it can now be discerned only by an overgrown cemetery and a historical plaque by the roadside. Lambert

Lewisia oppositifolia

Lewisia stebbinsii

eral well-being threatened by long drought periods, one wonders whether *L. stebbinsii* will manage to survive much longer. Its loss of habitat renders it among the most endangered of lewisias.

In a season of ample moisture, this small lewisia can carpet the ground with its lively mauve-and-white blooms. It then appears to be spreading outward in the drainage runnels of these serpentine screes. In drought years, however, it is difficult to find a single plant, let alone flowers. The plant may have made an initial attempt to grow, but without sustaining snowmelt, it has been forced into early dormancy without flowering. *Lewisia stebbinsii* can survive such conditions for several consecutive years, but certainly at great cost.

Lewisia stebbinsii grows profusely on nearly bald serpentine in the region of Hells Half-Acre, Mendocino National Forest, California JOHN MASSEY/PHILIP BAULK

The flowers of *Lewisia stebbinsii*, when they do appear, are very appealing, rather like a double-sized *L. pygmaea*, rosy mauve or fuchsia-pink with a bold white eye. The leathery leaves, rather few and disparate in size, form a distorted, loose rosette. The flowers face upward from the prostrate stalks on the mossy surface rubble; these stalks are cast off as the seed ripens.

In the shelter of a few somber, wind-pruned Shasta firs (*Abies magnifica* var. *shastensis*), knee-high tangles of bright green Brewer's oak (*Quercus garryana* var. *breweri*), and occasional bushes of *Ribes*, few low plants or even lichens survive on these ridges. Protected sites below the snowline support the elegant little fern *Cheilanthes gracillima*, and in coarse rubble there are occasional plants of *Penstemon purpusii*, with *Calyptridium quadripetalum* in crevices or colonizing freshly exposed soil. *Viola hallii* and the little olive-and-silver *Fritillaria glauca* and *F. purdyi*

can be seen, while *Erigeron delicatus*, miles south of its major populations, produces a lilac froth. The protective shrubs buffer the winds and create the snowbeds that give life to these tenacious little plants; most of the summits have no such snow cover.

Occasional rosettes of *Lewisia nevadensis* with typical white flowers appear in the snowbed habitat of the type area for *L. stebbinsii*. Rarely one finds an individual plant similar to *L. nevadensis* but with smooth lilac flowers and broader leaves, undoubtedly a hybrid of the two. There is also a pretty display of *L. triphylla* along the little melt rills.

From its slender rootstock and caudex, *Lewisia stebbinsii* produces very precocious leaves. The dormant resting bud

Lewisia stebbinsii, north of Hull Mountain in the Mendocino National Forest, California   SEAN HOGAN

is sheathed in dried leaf bases and stubs of flower stalks in a manner peculiar to this species. The flower stalk is usually longer than the foliage, but procumbent.

Though not easily grown, *Lewisia stebbinsii* has been cultivated in Britain and Europe since 1979. It is seldom seen in American collections.

Pygmaea Cluster

Lewisia glandulosa
(P. A. Rydberg) Dempster 1990

Lewisia glandulosa has remained a rather obscure member of the genus. It was first collected in 1902 on Mount Dana near Yosemite by Charles E. Hall and Ernest Babcock. Only a few stubborn systematic botanists and specialty growers have recognized the genuine plant; confusing introgression with the similar *Lewisia pygmaea* makes its identification problematic.

Rydberg (1932) christened this plant *Oreobroma glandulosum*; Roxanna Ferris (1944) reduced it to a subspecies of *Lewisia pygmaea*. It was restored to specific rank by Lauramay Dempster (1990), who believed it to be an ancestral source of *L. pygmaea*, which species she suggested had arisen through the hybridization of *L. glandulosa* with *L. nevadensis*, followed by ongoing introgression and backcrossing. Hershkovitz and Hogan plan to include it within *L. pygmaea* but concede that it may be a separate species.

Lewisia glandulosa differs from *L. pygmaea* in its very long, tapering root and small white flowers. It is common in the narrow zone between the treeline and the permanent snowfields, comprising tundra and associated snowbound fellfields—the most stable of the world's vegetational zones. Though apparently harsh, tundra offers benign security to a surprisingly broad range of plants. *Lewisia glandulosa* is known from the high Sierra Nevada, from the vicinity of Mount Conness and Mount Dana south to the Mount Whitney cluster of peaks; it also occurs in the adjacent White Mountains.

Lewisia glandulosa

Lewisia glandulosa is a long-lived cushion plant, technically deciduous although the previous year's parts persist as a mat of shrunken, ashy, marcescent tissue under the fresh foliage and flowering stems. One venerable herbarium specimen looked something like a tattered foliose lichen about one foot (30 cm) across; before it was collected it had exploded into a multitude of tiny blossoms, each one little larger than a pinhead on a pin-thin stalk—a wondrous jeweled pincushion. All this came from a root that must have been 2 inches (5 cm) in diameter when alive, as husky as that of the very different *L. congdonii*. This growth habit is in sharp contrast with that of *L. pygmaea*, which arises from a short, thick rootstock that does not probe deeply and is probably not very long-lived, in relative terms.

The epithet Rydberg chose this time characteristically calls attention to a detail, the glands. To the unaided eye, these glands register as a blur of color within the flower. With a lens, however, they are perceived as remarkable structures lining the margins of both bracts and sepals like minuscule stalked beads of amethyst glass. Their glistening color may entice tiny pollinating insects.

The lofty Sierran heights where *Lewisia glandulosa* dwells are not warmed until mid-July or later (earlier in the White Mountains). The short but brilliant growing season is abruptly terminated by frost in early fall. Young plants are so small they can be overlooked even in flower, except where they grow in masses along wet runnels. The larger veterans are found on nearby moist outcrops, where protection from erosion has allowed them to reach impressive dimensions.

These mature plants produce dozens of plane-bladed, narrowly lanceolate leaves annually from multiplex crowns, as well as a multitude of flowering stems.

Detail of *Lewisia glandulosa*

The leaves may reach a length of 4 inches (10 cm) in ideal conditions; usually they are much shorter. Each threadlike flowering stem bears one or two pairs of bracts above the midpoint, and two or three flowers per stalk, barely exceeding the leaves, if at all. The typical flower color is white, but pastels are sometimes seen, perhaps a result of introgression from other, pink-flowered species.

Lewisia glandulosa is all but unknown in cultivation. In the Pacific Northwest it has been reticent—not so accommodating as *L. longipetala* —but is showing some promise and a sprinkling of tiny white flowers.

Lewisia longipetala
(C. V. Piper) S. Clay 1937

How was it possible that a little plant from California, found there only once in 1875 and never known to be in cultivation, could suddenly appear in England almost sixty years later? This phenomenon occurred in 1934 when a lewisia flowered at the Royal Horticultural Society's garden at Wisley. Its seed source is not remembered, but it had probably arrived as *Lewisia pygmaea*, as the label indicated. The plant was pictured with Millard's March 1935 article for the *Journal of the Royal Horticultural Society*, but the April issue of the journal made clear that the pictured plant was the Wisley specimen. It was identified as *L. pygmaea*, although it was obviously atypical of that species, and its seed was gathered and distributed.

Another mysterious sighting of what was probably *Lewisia longipetala* is documented in a life-sized black-and-white photograph (credited to A. Nichols and captioned *L. nevadensis*) in *North American Rock Plants* (Preece 1937). It clearly shows the six to eight narrow, equal petals; the flowers are described as up to three per stem, opening in succession to starry, not oval, pink blossoms. The anthers are dark; the pollen was said to stain the petals faintly lavender. The description is unmistakably that of

Lewisia longipetala

L. longipetala, although Preece did not mention the sepals (green in *L. nevadensis* and without stalked glands). The foliage was deep green, not the yellowish green of *L. nevadensis*. A robust though small plant, it was said to be easily grown from the freely produced seed, often flowering within six months if sown early and producing a succession of flower stalks in as many as five flushes per season in the alpine house (only two or three in the open). When cool fall conditions set in, the plant became latently deciduous, as though hesitant about closing down for winter. Perhaps the seed came to Preece in Victoria, British Columbia, from the Wisley plants, or even from the collector who supplied Wisley.

In a photograph on page 49 of his monograph, Roy Elliott (1966) provisionally designated the plant featured as the "Lewisia 'pygmaea' of horticulture," whereupon American lewisia buffs, as well as members of the California Native Plant Society, snapped to attention and got out their maps. A fourth published photograph was taken by Margaret Williams in the wild, after the confusion was straightened out, and *Lewisia longipetala* was at last declared refound. This photograph appeared in the 1978 second edition of Elliott's monograph. Examination of the published photographs proves they are of the same species.

It was eventually determined that *Lewisia longipetala* must be a long-lost Sierran species first collected in 1875 by John G. Lemmon, an amateur botanist who had come to California in hope of regaining his health after surviving the horrors of Andersonville Prison during the Civil War. Settling in Sierraville as a schoolteacher, he spent his spare time studying and writing about the native plants and making herbarium collections with his wife in the northern Sierra Nevada and adjacent parts of Nevada. In summer 1875 he found an unfamiliar plant in the Sierra Nevada of California, somewhere "west of Truckee," according to his label. His collections were sent to the U.S. National Herbarium, where they lay neglected for decades until the arrival of Charles Vancouver Piper, who published this plant in 1913 as a new species, *Oreobroma longipetalum*.

Lewisia longipetala in the Sierra Nevada's Desolation Wilderness, west of Lake Tahoe SEAN HOGAN

In July 1967 G. Ledyard Stebbins refound Lemmon's lewisia, which had not been seen since its original collection, in several high-elevation sites in the Crystal Range about 40 miles (65 km) south of Truckee. The following season he and some companions, including Margaret and Loring Williams, found it west of Truckee in an area that would have been easily accessible to Lemmon as he traveled from Sierraville on horseback. "If this is not Lemmon's station, then it is very close to it," Stebbins (1968) wrote; he proposed the plant's transfer as *Lewisia longipetala*. Plant-hunters searched high and low in the peaks and canyons west of Truckee. All the occurrences known to date are within or immediately adjacent to the western rim of the Tahoe Basin of the northern Sierra Nevada, with Lemmon's station (it happens to be the northernmost) in the drainage of the Little Truckee River. In the 1978 second edition of his monograph, Elliott tentatively identified the "Lewisia 'pygmaea' of horticulture" as *L. longipetala*.

How, in the intervening decades, did seed of *Lewisia longipetala* come to Wisley? Lemmon collected no seed, and his probable site is readily accessible and lies only a short hike from the Donner Pass access road and the Southern Pacific Railway station and old hotel at the summit. It may well have been found here by the seed collector and writer Ellen Lester Rowntree, an expatriate Englishwoman who combed California from 1931 to 1945 in her old touring car.

Lester Rowntree (as she preferred to be called) was a well-known collector of the period, working from her home base at Carmel Highlands on the coast. A proto-feminist, she left behind her roles of wife and mother at fifty-three and set about building a new life totally on her own. The only compensation she received from her divorce was freedom. She commenced seed collecting as a full-time venture in 1931 and issued her first seed list in 1932, about the time that the *Lewisia longipetala* seed lot must have arrived at Wisley. She wrote of finding flowers above 10,000 feet (3050 meters), "way back in there where reflected light had brought them out"; and of once casting off her garments and dancing in a mountain downpour. Surely this is the kind of collector who might have happened onto Lemmon's lost lewisia!

Margaret Williams perfectly described *Lewisia longipetala* as having flowers the color of a strawberry ice-cream soda (which probably surprised the British, since the plant they know is white). These lively but cool blossoms are strikingly set off by a pair of maroon-purple sepals, sparkling with tiny glands. The plant is larger than the typical *L. pygmaea* in all respects, with longer leaves and larger flowers—as many as three per stalk, though Stebbins found them only in singles.

Where a deep, sparkling lake now lies high on the Sierra crest, a much higher plateau once stood, in a weather pattern that encouraged much snow and a huge Ice Age glacier. The lewisia is found in a limited number of colonies, and those are associated with the most persistent snowbanks, so intimately and inextricably is it bound to its circumstances. In years of heaviest snowfall the plants may never be released from winter's ice and go on to flower; in drought seasons without deep snow, the plants may simply burn out, parched.

Anne Halford photographed a colony on Keith's Dome in the Crystal Range on 11 July 1990. In this drought year, an estimated thousand plants were in flower, surviving from an ample snowmelt. Usually these were solitary and appeared to have longer petals than usual, as if in compensation for the paucity of flowers.

To return to England, a distinct variation of *Lewisia longipetala* is grown in the collection at Ashwood Nurseries by Philip Baulk, who received it from a now-forgotten source as *L. longiscarpa*. This form consistently has flowers with rounder petals and a much more pointed resting bud, so that it can easily be identified even during its winter dormancy.

Lewisia longipetala has proven to be a superior parent for small hybrid lewisias, invariably bestowing its musky fragrance to its offspring. The first was Will Ingwersen's 'Pinkie', a cross that is appreciated by even the most obstinate purist.

Lewisia nevadensis

(A. Gray) B. L. Robinson 1897

Lewisia nevadensis is quite appropriately called the lewisia of the snows. Not only is it found in the Sierra Nevada (Spanish for "snowy mountains"), but a meadow full of the tufts of this flower looks something like the aftermath of a light snowfall. This species is a stable and recognizable entity throughout its considerable range, but human error has muddled its identity and given it a less than enthusiastic following.

Lewisia nevadensis was first found by Sereno Watson on the King expedition in the eastern Humboldt (or Ruby) Mountains of Nevada in 1868; the following year Watson collected it in the Wasatch Range of Utah. Asa Gray formally published it as *Calandrinia nevadensis* in 1873, before these new plants from the West were satisfactorily sorted out. Gray later recognized that it could not be a *Calandrinia* because of the manner in which its capsule opened, so he transferred it as *L. nevadensis*. It was among the species Howell (1893) moved to his new genus *Oreobroma* and was returned to *Lewisia* when Robinson (1897) invalidated *Oreobroma*. Francis Fosberg (1942) transferred *L. nevadensis* Gray 1873 as *L. pygmaea* var. *nevadensis*, setting up an ongoing controversy about the relationship of these species; Lauramay Dempster (1990) restored its specific status.

Perhaps all this uncertainty contributed to a certain disdain in which it came to be held by gardeners. As Margaret Williams confided in a letter to Roy Elliott, "Because it is common, abundant and not distinguished, one remembers seeing [*Lewisia nevadensis*] often but not exactly where or when" (Elliott 1966). Ira Gabrielson (1932) noted that its petals were "so thin they make only a half-hearted attempt at being white." Nevertheless, this is quite a recognizable lewisia. Its extensive range includes a large portion of the western mountains. It often occurs with *L. triphylla*, and not uncommonly it shares the land with *L. pygmaea*, in which case taxonomically troubling intermediate swarms may be seen, as in the Warner Mountains of northeastern California.

Lewisia nevadensis

The snowy lewisia is found, appropriately enough, beneath snowbeds in stony, shallow seeps and springy turf, often among thin grasses and on cool northern exposures. Here the cold meltwater saturates the soil until summer is well advanced, encouraging flowering throughout the season. Companions in these wet habitats may include such miniature plants as *Hesperochiron*, *Dicentra uniflora*, *Parnassia*, *Ranunculus*, *Camassia*, sedges, and other seep lovers. In 1967 Gary Gurley, a correspondent from the vicinity of Washington's western Cascade foothills, called my attention to such a colony of *Lewisia nevadensis* in western Yakima County at 6000 to 7000 feet (1830 to 2130 meters), with a road through it. More than thirty years later, these approximately 2 square miles (5 sq km) remain a sight to see in late July through August in cooler summers, offering a myriad of snowy lewisias and a few *L. triphylla* but no *L. pygmaea*.

In spite of some disparagement by gardeners, *Lewisia nevadensis* has its good qualities. It grows readily in almost any suitably wet place where the

A superior form of *Lewisia nevadensis*, Siskiyou Mountains, Oregon AL HOBART

substrate allows free percolation—never stagnation. This humble plant has become something of a weed in some gardens, including the Rock Alpine Garden in Denver, where *L. pygmaea* can hardly be grown. At Askival, the garden of Polly and Mike Stone near the shores of Loch Lomond in Scotland, it self-seeds freely, as it also does in the Iceland garden of Olafur Gudmundsson, who testifies admiringly to its cheerful reliability. It is often possible to choose superior forms with flowers up to one inch (2.5 cm) across; a single such plant can produce hundreds of seedlings. I have seen inspiring herbarium specimens from such disparate sites as Idaho's Seven Devils Mountains, the Siskiyous of Oregon, and the headwaters of California's Feather River along the Pacific Crest Trail.

Lewisia nevadensis is a sparse plant compared to others of the *Pygmaea* cluster. The rosette is flatter and more nearly rosulate. Thick pedicels hold single terminal blossoms, with numerous stems produced in ideal conditions. Each 3-inch (7.5-cm) plant may become a little white nosegay over a long period.

The flower of *Lewisia nevadensis* is curiously unlike all other lewisias in being eccentric, or out of round. This is not an optical illusion but a real feature with some diagnostic value. At first it seems that the rigidity of the pair of sepals prevents the bud from opening fully, so that the flower is elliptic. Actually, the two petals affixed opposite the locus, where the sepals join, are both longer and broader than the other four to eight petals. The sepals are entire, but sometimes they have erose margins, as if nibbled by something with tiny teeth.

Now considered conspecific with *Lewisia nevadensis* is *L. bernardina*, published in 1921 by Anstruther Davidson, identifying a plant he found in cool seepages near Bear Lake in the San Bernardino Mountains of southern California. *Lewisia bernardina* was transferred as *Oreobroma bernardinum* and allied with *L. nevadensis* by Rydberg (1932). Fosberg (1942) transferred it as *L. pygmaea* var. *bernardina*. This plant has been grown abroad for many years and may have had something to do with the "brachycalyx impostor" recently offered by European growers and discussed under *L. brachycalyx*.

Lewisia nevadensis 'Rosea' has an interesting story. Henrik Zetterlund, curator of the Göteburg Botanical Garden's alpine section, found this completely charming little rose-colored treasure in a private Swedish garden; realizing its uniqueness, he passed it along in the best gardening tradition, and seed from the plant was distributed by the Göteburg Botanical Garden in 1986 and 1987. Zetterlund suspects that this selection may in fact be an allotetraploid hybrid, the result of a cross between *L. nevadensis* and *L. brachycalyx*.

Lewisia pygmaea
(A. Gray) B. L. Robinson 1897

Lewisia pygmaea was first collected by Henry Engelmann, who found it on Bridger's Pass (7532 feet; 2600 meters) while crossing the Continental Divide in Wyoming, later the route of the Union Pacific Railway. He sent a specimen to the herbarium of his brother George in Saint Louis. It was first described and published by Asa Gray in 1862, as *Talinum pygmaeum*, only because the distinctions among North American portulacads had not yet been well established. In 1868 George Engelmann's description of the plant was published as *Calandrinia pygmaea*, negating Gray's *Talinum*. In 1873 Gray too renamed the plant *C. pygmaea*.

Thomas Jefferson Howell (1893) annexed *Calandrinia pygmaea* to his genus *Oreobroma*, and when B. L. Robinson (1897) demolished that genus, our subject came into *Lewisia* with a number of its relatives.

The pygmy lewisia is among the smaller members of its genus. The plants appear more tufted than rosulate, and they seem to vary more in response to local enviromental factors from one season to another. The rootstock and caudex together are short and compact, either carrotlike or branched, and bear a small emergent bundle of leaves and flower stalks to-

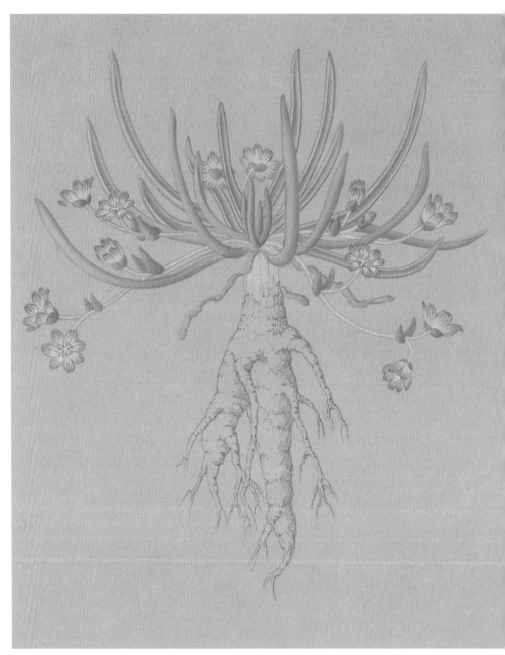

Lewisia pygmaea

gether in spring, as do others of its section. The numerous channeled leaves are rich green, often flushed with tannish purple. Fully mature plants bear many flowering stems, each with many flowers, which may continue to open until cut down by frost.

Lauramay Dempster offered a solution to the confusing nature of *Lewisia pygmaea* when she observed that matters would have been clearer had *L. glandulosa* been known as early as *L. pygmaea* and *L. nevadensis*, instead of being described more than half a century later. Dempster (1990) wrote:

> Since it is evident ... that *Lewisia pygmaea* blends on the one hand with *L. nevadensis* and on the other with *Oreobroma glandulosum* [*L. glandulosa*], the tendency has been to make the two extremes infraspecific taxa under *L. pygmaea*, the tacit assumption being that the variable and widespread *L. pygmaea* is the parent of the other two taxa. It seems clear to me however, that this is the wrong approach. *Lewisia nevadensis* and *O. glandulosum* are completely distinct and clearly different from each other. It is only the existence of *L. pygmaea* that blurs that distinction....Contrary to the tacit assumption mentioned above, my theory is that *L. pygmaea* is of hybrid origin, and is continually undergoing introgression from the other two species.

Lewisia pygmaea in Idaho
MARGARET WILLIAMS

Dempster considered two options: lumping all three taxa under one name—a temptation Mathew (1989) discussed and rejected; or "to recognize three species, two of which can be clearly defined, at least in relation to each other, the third, however, (*L. pygmaea*) being intermediate, widespread, variable and ill defined."

California botanists have often treated *Lewisia pygmaea* and *L. nevadensis* as a closely related pair of species. Francis Fosberg (1942), however, working with the extensive collections of the U.S. National Herbarium, decided that "the differences between the two have been given much more importance than they deserve"; he concluded that they should be treated as a single species, *L. pygmaea*, with two varieties, *pygmaea* and *nevadensis*.

The possibility of hybrid origin deserves careful consideration. It frequently occurs that two species become bridged by a continuous exchange of genetic material; through a great many generations, the hybrid populations assume a distinct character of their own. Moreover, the newcomers may be markedly more tolerant of a broad range of environmental conditions, allowing them to expand their range into fresh territory where their parents never existed. Whatever its origin, *Lewisia pygmaea* behaves exactly as a strong, aggressive species should: it occupies a greater range than any other member of its genus, and it displays a perplexing array of variation.

It is likely that during the Pleistocene glaciation, when mean sea level was as much as 300 feet (90 meters) lower than at present, *Lewisia pygmaea* found a migration track along the Pacific Front, where it advanced north to the ice-free Yukon Valley of Alaska and inland from there into the Yukon Basin in Canada. It now occurs intermittently along the Coast Range of British Columbia, in the Saint Elias Range near the Alaskan border, and in the Alaska Range at the base of Denali; it may perhaps occur in the Brooks Range, though there are no reports of it from that vast wilderness. At the same time, the incipient species spread over many other western ranges: the Sierra Nevada and Cascades, and through the Rockies northeast to Alberta and south to Arizona. It is found on Vancouver Island and the Olympic Peninsula of Washington, but not in the Coast Ranges to the south, where it is to some extent replaced by *L. nevadensis*.

One factor that undoubtedly contributes to the success of *Lewisia pygmaea*, and perhaps others of this section, is its preference for seasonally wet sites. Here plants can grow rapidly, sometimes germinating, flowering, and setting seed in a single season, like annuals. If moisture is available throughout the summer, these lewisias can remain in flower until shut down by frost.

On 5 August 1935 Roxanna Ferris and a companion collected a diminutive plant at Martha Lake in the headwaters of the San Joaquin River at nearly 11,000 feet (3355 meters), well above timberline; she published it as *Lewisia sierrae* (Ferris 1944). In my opinion, Ferris's plant is better considered a variant of *L. pygmaea*; it is only about half the size of *L. pygmaea* and occupies a well-defined territory, from the Tahoe Basin in Nevada south to Olancha Peak near Mount Whitney in the southern Sierra Nevada, where it impressed John Thomas Howell during his extensive surveys of the highest aeries of the Whitney cluster of peaks. It is a plant of higher elevations; at its lower limits it sometimes grows with typical *L. pygmaea* and *L. nevadensis* (as well as *L. triphylla*), but it apparently does not consort with *L. glandulosa*. It is adapted to dry, turfy knolls and slopes, where there is no competition or shade from larger plants, and the short grasses stabilize the loose, rocky substrate, trap warmth, and produce humus. Here the lewisias find the good seedbeds they need to flourish during the brief wet growing season below the snowbeds.

Dempster (1993) considered the Sierra lewisia the slightest and highest-dwelling of the many variants of *L. pygmaea*; she entirely sank it into *L. pygmaea*, and I have reflected this in my classification. Because the Sierra lewisia is stable, however, with established discrete populations, I believe it is a particularly adapted segregant within the species. Morphologically, it is distinct in that its sepals lack any glandular dentation. In some populations (as at Mount Rose in Nevada), the foliage is quietly colorful, making the tiny tuffets conspicuous amid the thin grasses; the leaves are a hearty olive-green, with the least exposed parts blanched to the color of wheatstraw and the margins touched with bright gold and

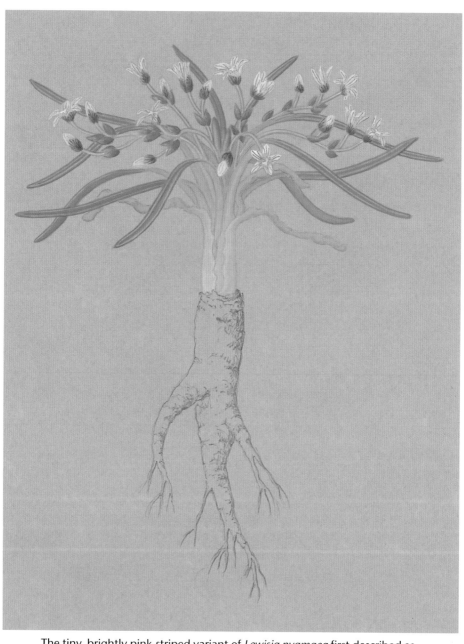

The tiny, brightly pink-striped variant of *Lewisia pygmaea* first described as *L. sierrae*

ocher. This is a charming foil to the tiny white flowers emblazoned with bright pink venation.

The Sierra lewisia has been grown by a few European collectors since about 1975, and several forms are occasionally available commercially, including one with attractively colored foliage. In its North American homeland, however, it is little known to gardeners.

Lewisia pygmaea, perhaps more than any other lewisia, has produced a great variety of singular colonies with striking flower colors. Seed gathered, grown, and selected from such populations could produce worthy garden strains. The name 'Apache Doll' was given to a distinct color form of *L. pygmaea* introduced by Sonia Lowzow Collins from Crescent Lake, Apache County, in Arizona's White Mountains. It has flowers of vibrant cerise with a pale eye that appears almost white by contrast.

Lewisia pygmaea 'Apache Doll' in its native habitat, Arizona's White Mountains
BURL MOSTUL

Subgenus *Strophiolum*

In the monotypic subgenus *Strophiolum*, the plant releases its seeds in a manner that is quite distinct among the Portulacaceae. Most portulacads have seed capsules that open in an apically valvate manner, splitting from the top downward along the longitudinal valves, or seams (usually three), to the base of the capsule; the resulting three sections of the capsule top remain in place, attached at the base. In *Lewisia*, and a few other portulacads, this rupture begins at the bottom—what is termed circumscissile dehiscence—following an almost imperceptible suture around the capsule at the base. This occurs as the capsule dries out and shrinks, while the seeds ripen. The top portion of the capsule is cast off as a single unit. The single exception is *Lewisia tweedyi*, in which the initial splitting occurs while the capsule is still turgid (not dried and shrunken). The capsule splits downward along the valves to the base, revealing the seed still firmly attached to the columnar placenta. As the capsule dries, the circumscissile rupture takes place, with the top portion falling away in tatters. The seeds are shed later, often loosened by ants as the insects feed on the strophiolar pulp.

The designation *Strophiolum* alludes to the strophiole, a prominent fleshy appendage at the outer end of the seed. Janet Hohn (1975) proposed a section of this name to accommodate the single species *Lewisia tweedyi*, and the name was validated as a subgenus by Brian Mathew (1989).

Following the lead of J. Linn Bogle, Roger Carolin, and others in attempts to improve the taxonomy of the Portulacaceae, Mark Hershkovitz, then at the University of California, Davis, concentrated on the genus *Calandrinia*, which had become something of a catch-all. Working with others, Hershkovitz recommended a thorough reevaluation of this genus, including the reinstatement of the subgenus *Cistanthe* to its original status as a genus. To this genus he transferred a number of western North American portulacads, including *Lewisia tweedyi*, the entire genus *Calyptridium*, and the allied *Spraguea* (Hershkovitz 1990).

Doctoral research at the University of Washington by Janet Hohn (1975) disclosed undeniable evidence that Tweedy's lewisia lay outside the phylogenetic mainstream of the genus, while at the same time, it showed strong affinities with the other *Lewisia* species she was studying. Hershkovitz (1990), using slightly different criteria, discerned equally convincing affinities with *Cistanthe*. He later conceded, however, that *Lewisia tweedyi* was quite unlike other members of *Cistanthe* and has mused that it might be viewed as belonging equally to *Cistanthe* and *Lewisia*, or that it might even be transferred once again from the genus *Cistanthe* into a new monotypic genus (pers. comm. 1999).

Mathew (1989) had considered it best retained as a *Lewisia* species, the type of subgenus *Strophiolum*, but later allowed that *Lewisia tweedyi* might best be placed in a monotypic genus yet to be described (pers. comm. 1997). Hohn too notes that further study might warrant the creation of a new monotypic genus for *L. tweedyi* (Hohn 1975).

Lewisia tweedyi
(A. Gray) B. L. Robinson 1897
[Cistanthe tweedyi (A. Gray) Hershkovitz 1990]

Lewisia tweedyi was discovered by Frank Tweedy while he was working with T. S. Brandegee on a government railway survey in the wilds of Washington Territory in the Wenatchee Range, near Mount Stuart, in August 1882. Asa Gray (1887) named it for him as *Calandrinia tweedyi*, and thence it followed a well-worn taxonomic path for lewisias discovered in the late nineteenth century: having been described as a species of *Calandrinia* (Gray 1887), it was briefly separated into *Oreobroma* (Howell 1893); transferred with section *Pachyrhiza* of that genus into *Lewisia* (Robinson 1897); and returned with all *Oreobroma* to *Lewisia* (Rydberg 1932). There it rested, garnering the admiration of wildflower lovers and gardeners alike, until the work of Hohn (1975) and Hershkovitz (1990), just described.

Lewisia tweedyi

One of the most arresting of all western wildflowers, Tweedy's lewisia is almost a legend in the mountains where it grows. Everyone wants to find it, photograph it, and possess it. Its staunch foliage is a husky foil for the large bowl-shaped, nodding blossoms, up to three or four in succession on each flowering stem, looming out of the mossy rocks. The usual colors are those of apricots, peaches, citrus fruits, and melons, but occasionally one sees a pastel blush, ivory, or crushed strawberry hue. Rosy strains have been selected in cultivation, as well as white ones.

Tweedy's lewisia is a palpable remnant of the preglacial flora from a time before the Cascade Ranges had developed, and before the devastation of the Ice Ages, of course. It is now found principally within the We-

Lewisia tweedyi thriving on Chumstick Mountain, Entiat Ridge, in Washington's Wenatchee Mountains JACK POFF

natchee Mountains of central Washington, with sporadic occurrences northward into British Columbia. The Wenatchee Mountains consist of several long southeasterly granitic ridges of the North Cascades, with their drainages mainly through the Entiat and Wenatchee rivers to the Columbia south from Lake Chelan. These geologically complex mountains support a flora different from that of the rest of the Cascades. The unglaciated, relatively low ridges of the Wenatchee Mountains are separated from one another by precipitous canyons; a cover of ponderosa pine and Douglas fir is interspersed with broad grassland slopes, indicating a long history of range fires. The canyons open southeasterly onto the Columbia Plateau, a great basalt flow with a continental, semiarid climate.

In 1950 a nature writer wrote that to see *Lewisia tweedyi*, one need only go to the Wenatchee Mountains and take any road leading to an abandoned gold mine. Those dusty roads are still there, and so are the tunnels and tailing piles from the old mines. The lewisia is still there too, but like the gold, it is not so easy to come by; nonetheless, it has had something of

Lewisia tweedyi 'Elliott's Variety', a superior selection grown by Ashwood Nurseries JOHN MASSEY/PHILIP BAULK

a come-back in recent years. It was known to the old-time locals as the mountain rose and still answers to that name in the Wenatchees.

The plants grow on slopes in an arid soil that is cooled by its own porosity, freely exchanging oxygen and water vapor with the atmosphere. These scree soils have accumulated to great depths on the steep slopes because no soil was ever removed by glaciation, and little is washed away by precipitation in this dry climate. The soils are derived from frost shattering of the parent rock and are unstructured, conglomerate heaps, with the finest particles having been carried off by wind to lodge elsewhere. These screes are open, breathing soils with considerable humus from conifers and grasses.

Vigorous and floriferous clumps of *Lewisia tweedyi* stand out in the arid austerity of Entiat Ridge SEAN HOGAN

Moraine soils such as those from the Mount Stuart glaciation, however, have been sorted by meltwater. The coarser portions provide conditions favorable to *Lewisia tweedyi*, and it has become established in the canyons of both Icicle and Ingalls creeks, which were once occupied by the Stuart glaciers. This species has crept northward into many similar places in the centuries since the retreat of the glaciers.

Lewisia tweedyi succeeds perhaps because of the adversities of its habitat rather than in spite of them. Its broad, soft leaves are only temporarily affected by the sharp temperature reversals of the continental climate and the desiccating winds. Though it may be harmed, it survives even without a protective blanket of snow. It does well in valleys and canyons at around 1700 feet (570 meters), where precipitation is as little as 8 inches (20 cm), and on ridgetop summits to 7000 feet (2350 meters), where as much as 20 inches (50 cm) of precipitation falls, mostly as snow. Summer showers here occur only sporadically, but occasional cloudbursts are not unknown. Summer afternoons are scorching, but the heat is dispelled by the sharp night cooling of arid lands and frequent dew.

Lewisia tweedyi's bold, glossy clumps of foliage are a surprise in its austere setting. It is most prominent in forest openings, where it grows wedged among cooling rocks even in high shade. Unlike other lewisias, it persists even when the forest becomes a closed canopy, although it does not flower in such reduced light. When the trees are cut, blown down, or burned, these sites swarm with flowers the following spring.

Over the years as a forest matures, vigorous plants reach for light, extending rhizomes slowly across the surface, rooting as they go. I saw one small colony near the base of a large old ponderosa pine. The tree was collapsing from age, exposing the ground to the sunlight, and the corky old multi-branched shell of the lewisia rootstock remained to tell the story of its long struggle. A friend of mine once salvaged from a collapsed roadbank a venerable plant with a tap-rooted caudex 8 feet (2.5 meters) long and 8 inches (20 cm) in diameter below the crown: the roots of *Lewisia tweedyi* plunge widely and deeply for moisture.

Range fires frequently pass over the habitat of *Lewisia tweedyi*. As I write this, a November fire has just covered 600 acres (240 hectares) of its range on the north slopes below Mission Ridge in the Wenatchee Range, but the lewisias will probably benefit from it. Fire is not a problem for the species, but human interference can be. Bulldozing to create firebreaks can devastate lewisia colonies irreparably.

At this time we can expect that *Lewisia tweedyi* will continue to survive as it has through millennia. The Washington State Department of Natural Resources Natural Heritage Program has classified it as a monitored species, meaning that though it is not quite ready for listing as rare, threatened, or endangered, it is being closely watched for habitat degradation and overharvesting of the seed.

The mature seed of Tweedy's lewisia smells of honey. Ants once carried off newly cleaned *Lewisia tweedyi* seed from a saucer on my worktable, leaving untouched the seeds of other lewisias right beside it. Apparently the strophiolar tissue attracts the ants, which consume it alone, leaving the seed itself unconsumed and more favorably relocated. Ants in the wild have been observed engaging in the same behavior. Nothing suggests that they store the seeds of *L. tweedyi* in caches; rather, they carry it a little distance, eat the strophiolar tissue, and discard the rest. This strategy, employed by many plants worldwide, is obviously advantageous in dispersing the plant to new sites, where the seedlings will not have to compete with their parents. The seed of *L. tweedyi* does not, it is true, travel as far as that of wind-assisted lewisias such as *L. leeana* or *L. rediviva*. Nonetheless, its seed is likely to remain on suitable soil in hospitable surroundings, increasing the colony slowly but steadily.

The earliest record of cultivation of *Lewisia tweedyi* is its flowering at Kew in May 1898, from material received from Columbia Nurseries of Astoria, Oregon. The Kew plants were featured in *Curtis's Botanical Magazine* in 1899. Carl Purdy enjoyed recalling the sensation created by the plants he sent to England around 1905; the horticultural press hailed *L. tweedyi* as "the greatest acquisition of a lifetime" and "among the four best alpines of the entire world" (the other three were not named). In 1975, an informal poll of American rock gardeners revealed *L. tweedyi* to be their favorite subject, though for most of them that seems to have been wishful thinking.

Despite its resistance to cultivation, *Lewisia tweedyi* is still coveted, a star of hope and desire in the eyes and hearts of gardeners. Nurseryman Steve Doonan of Issaquah, Washington, who has known this queen of plants for half a lifetime in the wild and in the garden, wonders how it can survive annual temperature extremes of ⁻25° and 100°F (⁻32° and 38°C) in the wild yet be so temperamental in captivity. The answer lies in the atmosphere: the plant's need for aridity is second only to its need for sunlight. Aridity is what makes the climate of the West distinctive; this lack of humidity is most noticeable in high summer. Another climatic condition that may affect the well-being of *L. tweedyi* is autumnal rainfall; there seems to be a correlation between such a seasonal dousing and colonies of large (and presumably old and permanent) plants. Plants take some time to recover from the stress of summer, first regaining the plumpness of their leaves and then replacing damaged absorptive roots. Only then can they resume their normal growth cycle and initiate flower buds.

One problem faced by growers is the reluctance of *Lewisia tweedyi* to set seed in cultivation. G. H. Berry, one of England's most venerated alpine specialists, built a fine stock from both cuttings and seed but gathered little seed even with the persistent effort of hand-pollination—none at all in some years (Berry 1952). Berry was also the first to point out that if there were no buds in autumn, there would be no flowers in spring. He was one of the first to note pink color in the species and passed propagules freely to friends, which in time may have netted the present pink strains of cultivation.

Attempts at pollination in cultivation may be ineffective for several reasons. In high humidity and/or low temperatures, the pollen may not ripen to the fine, waxy powder stage that marks its time of greatest fertility, or the stigma may not develop the sticky surface that indicates it is receptive, as Berry had deduced. In wild plants seed is produced plentifully each season, though not by every flower. Mature flowers picked in the wild can even ripen good seed if kept in a bottle of water on a windowsill!

Lewisia tweedyi has been a smashing garden success almost nowhere but in its natural range. In the side yard of a house in Leavenworth, Washington, a magnificent old plant, staunch as rhubarb, opens as many as five hundred flowers each season. Not far outside that little Cascade town, Coleman Leuthy has found the lewisia self-reliant in the garden, growing among substantial anchoring rocks in the cooling downdrafts off Entiat Ridge and Chumstick Mountain. He waters only if there has been little snowfall; as much as 4 feet (1.2 meters) of snow falls there in a normal year.

In the seasonally wet and usually humid Puget Sound trough of western Washington, Mareen S. Kruckeberg maintains a suitable environment for *Lewisia tweedyi* amid dryland ferns in an unheated alpine house. Rick Lupp succeeds in similar conditions further south. At my garden in Bellevue, Washington, the heavy, cold winter atmosphere dictates minimal watering to the plants, which I grow in containers under the sheltering eaves; unfortunately this results in minimal bud development. Those I have moved to a more favorable site on a vertical tufa wall have fared better. Far to the north, Aline Strutz wondered how seed was moved uphill to her Anchorage, Alaska, strawberry bed, where welcome lewisia seedlings had to be weeded out regularly—ants may have been the agent.

In the open, muggy summers of eastern Pennsylvania, Norman Deno finds the northwest exposure beneath the broad

Lewisia tweedyi in late May, Icicle Canyon, near Leavenworth, Washington SEAN HOGAN

eaves of his house a hospitable site for *Lewisia tweedyi*. His plants, in a deep sand bed, are given only an occasional light watering during spring growth—and total neglect for the other ten months of the year. In Ontario, where the snow lies long and deep, Barry Porteous has no difficulty growing this lewisia as long as it is planted horizontally on a steep slope; otherwise it is prone to decay at the caudex. *Lewisia tweedyi* tolerates his mulch of limestone chips, though *L. cotyledon* does not at all.

At 7000 feet (2130 meters) in Colorado, Andrew Pierce enjoys a spectacular show of both colored and white *Lewisia tweedyi*, grown with no special attention among *L. cotyledon* on a dry north-facing stone wall. In the nearly frost-free maritime fog belt in Eureka, California, Steven Darington could not succeed with *L. tweedyi*, and Sean Hogan, 300 miles (480 km) to the south in Berkeley, recorded that this species was the most disheartening in his extensive lewisia collection there.

In reviewing these reports, it is easy to surmise that snow and *Lewisia tweedyi* simply go together—but that is not the whole story. It may be tempting to brand this as one of those species so precisely adapted to particular environmental conditions that they will not readily settle into cultivation, but this dictum has been proven wrong for one plant after another. Observing how gardeners in different regions have succeeded should bring a bit of hope to aspiring growers of this sumptuous lewisia.

CHAPTER FIVE

Hybrids

ATURALISTS once believed that no wild species was capable of exchanging genetic material with another species. This concept of species became obsolete as people recognized that such crosses had always happened, whether spontaneously, in the wild or garden plot, or through planned human agency. Eventually hybridity came to be understood as a normal part of the process of speciation; within *Lewisia*, however, isolation and environmental factors have probably been more influential than hybridization in the differentiation of the species we now know.

Hybridity is not generally common in wild lewisia populations simply because they do not often occupy common ground; each species tends to be isolated from the others by its particular habitat preferences. This does not mean that suspected hybrids are not often noted in the literature or found among herbarium specimens. It is well to be cautious before assuming an anomalous lewisia is a hybrid: such characteristics as unusual flower color or leaf shape are encountered as natural variations in many populations. For example, just because a cotyledon hybrid has flowers of elegant apricot is no reason to suppose that *Lewisia tweedyi* was involved in its ancestry.

Plants that occupy the same area are said to be sympatric. Wherever two species of *Lewisia* are sympatric, we wonder whether they might possibly hybridize. Rarely a unique individual is found, so different that it appears to be evidence of such interbreeding. Sometimes the suspect individual is not only intermediate in many ways between the two species; it also appears to be seed-sterile, incapable of perpetuating itself. This is very good evidence of hybridity. Hybrid lewisias developed in cultivation are almost all sterile; exceptions are a partially fertile cross reported by Bedrich Parizek of the Czech Republic (*Lewisia cotyledon* × *L. columbiana*) and occasional individuals of *L.* ×*whiteae*.

In a small wilderness area in the Marble Mountains, no fewer than four distinct lewisias grow together—*Lewisia leeana*, *L. cotyledon*, *L. nevadensis*, and *L. triphylla*—as well as the hybrid *L.* ×*whiteae*. Another sympatric quartet, reported from the northern Sierra Nevada, includes *L. longipetala*, *L. pygmaea*, *L. nevadensis*, and *L. triphylla*; here there is no hint of interbreeding.

Sympatric trios are also uncommon. *Lewisia triphylla* and *L. nevadensis* keep company with *L. stebbinsii* on a serpentine ridgetop of California's northern Coast Range, along with an infrequent oddity, found in Mendocino County, California, in 1989, which seems to be a natural hybrid of *L. nevadensis* and *L. stebbinsii*. In the Wenatchee Mountains of Washington, *L. rediviva* and *L. tweedyi* are sometimes shoulder to shoulder, with *L. columbiana* only a short bee-flight away; again, however, there are no suspicious-looking offspring. There are surely many similar instances, but in general each *Lewisia* species keeps to itself. Sympatry does not suggest a genetic relationship but merely common environmental needs and tolerances.

Remarkably, given their relatively clear-cut distributional ranges, many *Lewisia* species have proven capable of interbreeding in cultivation. When species that are allopatric (found separated by considerable distances) are brought together in the garden or laboratory, limited genetic exchange may occur. The resulting hybrids rarely perpetuate themselves beyond a single generation and are of no botanical significance, but the occasional success affords a thrill for enthusiasts.

For some reason, reciprocal cross-pollination may not yield similar re-

Lewisia leeana and *L. cotyledon* hybridize readily wherever their ranges overlap, as in this healthy population of *L.* ×*whiteae* at Devils Punchbowl in the Siskiyous
PHYLLIS GUSTAFSON

sults; sometimes it results in fertile seed in one direction but not in the other. Attempts to pollinate *Lewisia cotyledon* with pollen from *L. leeana* have been largely fruitless, while the opposite cross (*L. leeana* × *L. cotyledon*) regularly yields seed, both in the wild and in the laboratory. (According to custom, the first name listed in a cross is the seed, or female, parent, and the second, the pollen, or male, parent.) This is apparent in natural colonies, where the hybrid individuals are found adjacent to and downslope from *L. leeana*. No other pair of species has been so thoroughly examined, but this example suggests further investigation should be encouraged.

Scientists, commercial horticulturalists, and backyard pollen-daubers have been instrumental in developing hybrid lewisias—and the bees have done their part, too. Some of the resulting plants have been cultivated for fifty years or more, a tenacity not common to this genus under garden conditions. These sturdy hybrids, adaptable to a wider range of conditions than their parents, have gained their fair share of horticultural recognition, including several awards.

Hybrid vigor in itself is not enough reason to grow hybrids, though it is certainly to be valued. We must be looking for qualities not already available in existing plants. Ease of cultivation, resistance to predators, and ease of vegetative propagation are all desirable. At the same time we want something novel, in particular clearer colors in a broader range— clean yellows, pristine lilacs, true reds and purples, and sharply contrasting bitones. We already have hybrids of miniature habit, bearing a profusion of flowers over a long period. One quality that has been somewhat overlooked is fragrance; selected plants of *Lewisia brachycalyx*, *L. longipetala*, and *L. rediviva* 'Henry Grant' possess scents ranging from delicate to musky.

Some growers, often termed "species purists," question whether we should be growing hybrids at all when the natural species offer such an abundance of beauty. This is entirely a matter of taste. The enthusiast who seeks out rare plants in the wild may experience momentary revulsion on being confronted with a sales table of three hundred lewisias in every tint and size, in a chemically induced paroxysm of bloom. Yet he or she should recall that the existence of these garden forms in no way threatens or diminishes the value of the true species; indeed, it is far better that the amateur gardener should take home a commercial hybrid that has a chance to survive in less than ideal conditions than a specialized plant that will soon decline and perish.

Probably the most remarkable hybrid lewisias have come from the mating of deciduous *Lewisia rediviva* with evergreen species. In every cross involving the bitterroot, the flowers are quite adequate, though of course sterile, and the foliage of most persists through the summer. Some have elongated, pointed, deciduous leaves, but for the most part they behave as if they had had only evergreen ancestors. This suggests that the evergreen pattern is ancestral, the deciduous pattern having been adopted to survive as the environment became warmer and drier.

A group, or grex (plural, greges), comprises all hybrids originating from the same parents or series of parents—regardless of which species was the pollen parent and which was the seed parent—but whose individuals vary in details of appearance, by which they may be recognized. Each hybrid may bear its own cultivar name in addition to the grex identification. The concept of a grex has permitted better understanding and appreciation of the vast array of hybrids involving *Saxifraga porophylla*, for instance, and the same should be possible for hybrid lewisias. Although it is difficult or impossible to identify hybrid greges by using a key, such as is applied to species, the practiced eye can discern certain characteristics shared by parents and offspring.

In the truest sense hybrid lewisias are those derived from parents of different species, not those derived from various phases or forms of a single species, nor the myriad garden forms of *Lewisia cotyledon*. The discussion of known hybrid lewisias offered in this chapter includes both spontaneous hybrids that have been found in the wild and deliberate and spontaneous hybrids produced in cultivation. I have gathered this material from many sources, some authenticated and others merely presumed, including nursery catalogs, botanical and horticultural journals, show reports, herbarium records, unpublished theses, and personal correspondence. In order to be of any value, this bulk of information had to be reduced to some sort of order; therefore I have organized this chapter cross by cross, assigning each named hybrid to a grex, according to its known or presumed parentage. On the whole, I have made no effort to distinguish which phase of *Lewisia cotyledon* was involved in a given cotyledon hybrid, nor have I known in each instance which plant was the seed parent and which the pollen donor. Finally, although few of these greges are represented by living plants, they are nonetheless a part of lewisia history. Each year, more and more of the survivors turn up in specialist catalogs and on show tables.

Lewisia brachycalyx × *L. columbiana* var. *rupicola.* This cross has been made in Europe, with the goal of obtaining mauve or violet flowers in small plants.

Lewisia brachycalyx × *L. cotyledon.* One of the earlier hybrid combinations, first made in England, these lewisias are easy, floriferous, and charming little evergreen plants. They tend to be short-lived, perhaps because they flower so freely. An exception is the earliest known hybrid—the first lewisia cross made by British grower Joe Elliott around 1950, and one he never bettered—'Phyllellia', named for his mother, Phyllis Elliott. The pollen came from the prizewinning cultivar *Lewisia cotyledon* var. *howellii* 'Weald Rose'. 'Phyllellia' forms a tidy 2-inch (5-cm) rosette of rather narrow leaves and bears a profusion of flowers from spring until fall. They are a rather incandescent rose with lines of crushed strawberry. The blossoms, one inch (2.5 cm) wide, are poised singly on short stems, appearing to float just above the leaves. The plant

Lewisia 'Phyllellia', the result of a cross between *L. brachycalyx* and *L. cotyledon*, garnered hybridizer Joe Elliott much-deserved praise JOHN MASSEY/PHILIP BAULK

Ashwood Nurseries made this happy cross of *Lewisia brachycalyx* and a pink hybrid of *L. cotyledon*; the unnamed result recalls *L.* 'Phyllellia', suffused with pink
JOHN MASSEY/PHILIP BAULK

looks like a superb, rosy *L. brachycalyx*. 'Phyllellia' received a Preliminary Commendation when first shown in 1951; an Award of Merit was bestowed on 12 May 1972 upon a specimen grown by Mrs. E. Ivey in Scotland. Using pollen from *L. cotyledon* var. *heckneri*, Elliott also produced 'Brachyheck', a nice enough plant when first introduced in the 1960s but now eclipsed.

Other reports of this grex come from Kath Dryden; from Bedrich Parizek; and from Fritz Kummert, an active hybridizer of *Lewisia* in Austria, who obtained a wide range of colors depending on the hue of the cotyledon parent. Parizek notes that seeds of large size tend to produce superior hybrid plants with a good color range and long season, but that these plants do not offset well for vegetative propagation. The few that do offset seem to exhaust themselves with the effort, never regaining their original vigor.

Bob Putnam, near Seattle, Washington, was fortunate in having pollen of *Lewisia cotyledon* var. *howellii* 'Carroll Watson' available to cross with *L. brachycalyx*. The resulting hybrid population first flowered in 1979, displaying a range of yellow tints from buckskin and saffron to creamy lemon chiffon. For many years, Steven Darington observed progeny raised from large-flowered cotyledon plants crossed with *L. brachycalyx*; he noted many large brachycalyx-like flowers, several times a season, early to late, on semideciduous symmetrical intermediate rosettes.

Lewisia brachycalyx × *L. longipetala*. Brian Mathew (1989) reported that hybrids from this cross were raised by Kath Dryden in England.

Lewisia brachycalyx × *L. oppositifolia*. Reported by Mathew (1989) as having been raised by Kath Dryden.

Lewisia brachycalyx × *L. pygmaea*. Kath Dryden reported obtaining a range of hybrids when the true *Lewisia brachycalyx* was crossed with the form of *L. pygmaea* grown in British gardens under the erroneous name *L. brachycalyx*. She wrote, "They do not live long but are a joy whilst they are alive."

Lewisia cantelovii × *L. columbiana* var. *rupicola.* This cross was reported by Leonard Wiley of Portland, Oregon. The plants were unflowered when he wrote, and he died shortly thereafter; I know nothing of the outcome. Steven Darington repeated the cross with the expected results: small-statured plants with intermediate characteristics.

Lewisia cantelovii × *L. columbiana* var. *wallowensis.* Sean Hogan raised a plant from this cross that appears promising. Steven Darington has also grown a small population of these hybrids, which he reported were not particularly vigorous.

Lewisia cantelovii × *L. cotyledon.* Leonard Wiley reported having made this cross, hoping to combine the profuse flowering of *Lewisia cantelovii* with larger flowers in a wider range of colors; nothing is known of his plants. A spontaneous seedling at Phil Pearson and Steve Doonan's Grand Ridge Nursery near Seattle seems to be just what Wiley had in mind; its flowers are lilac-tinted. A Dutch seed house has offered seed of this parentage with the brief description, "Dark rose, May-June, 20 cm"; if this is good seed set on an F_1 hybrid plant, it is a genuine breakthrough.

Lewisia cantelovii × *L. leeana.* Janet E. Hohn obtained five seeds from eleven crosses with *Lewisia leeana* as the seed parent. The reciprocal cross produced twenty-four seeds from seventeen pollinations, with several clones of both species being used. None of the resulting hybrids are known to survive.

Lewisia columbiana var. *columbiana* × *L. cantelovii.* This is a potentially interesting combination to produce durable, floriferous hybrids. Hohn obtained seed from the cross, but no plants are known to survive.

Lewisia columbiana var. *columbiana* × *L. columbiana* var. *rupicola.* Carl English made this cross to ascertain the breeding behavior of the two taxa as compared, for example, with the results obtained by crossing various cotyledon hybrids. In 1932 he named the result of this cross for his wife; according to the rules of horticultural nomenclature, it should now be known as *L.* ×*edithae* 'Edith English'. A variety of plants are sold in the Pacific Northwest under the name *L.* ×*edithae,* with the × often omitted.

This appears to be one of the sturdiest, easiest lewisias for the garden. Unprotected in the open, it was not damaged by subfreezing weather in the winter of 1978–1979 at Grand Ridge and went on with its usual show of salmon-pink flowers the following June to October. Late flower stalks always abort, giving rise to side rosettes on the tall stalks rather than bloom. Cuttings propagated over winter are highly successful.

The fact that *Lewisia* ×*edithae* does not produce seed led English to believe that its parents are distinct species. I too am tempted to regard them as such.

Lewisia columbiana var. *columbiana* × *L. columbiana* var. *wallowensis.* This grex comprises what appear to be introgressive individuals in populations in the Imnaha drainage in eastern Oregon, particularly at the Granny View Overlook on Grizzly Ridge. Seed has been collected from these plants, and the results are well represented in cultivation. The two paler plants of *Lewisia columbiana* var. *wallowensis* illustrated in Plate 8 of *The Genus Lewisia* (Mathew 1989) appear to belong here and may have been grown from seed taken at Granny View.

Lewisia columbiana var. *columbiana* × *L. leeana.* With *Lewisia columbiana* var. *columbiana* as seed parent, Hohn obtained 140 seeds from sixty-five attempts; from the reciprocal cross she got only twenty-four seeds in thirty attempts. Hers was an academic study and the plants were not grown on. Both Jane McGary and David Hale report having plants grown from this cross by Jim Baggett of Corvallis, Oregon. They have short, flattish leaves and deep rose flowers on very short, semierect stems.

***Lewisia columbiana* var. *wallowensis* × *L. columbiana* var. *rupicola*.** Darington has reported obtaining plants from this cross, made in both directions. Many have occurred spontaneously as well as deliberately; most resemble a more open-rosetted *Lewisia columbiana* var. *rupicola*, with smaller flowers.

***Lewisia cotyledon* × *L. columbiana* var. *columbiana*.** Unrecognized hybrids of this grex have occurred in many gardens where the parents have been grown together. Durable and floriferous, these have sometimes been assigned such names as "heckneri minor" or "howellii minor" based on their leaf forms and smaller flowers. Will Ingwersen cataloged one as 'Old Rose', and 'Wheatley's Variety' was once in commerce. Hohn obtained plentiful seed using many forms of both species, and Darington too had plants under observation. Parizek observed that with *Lewisia cotyledon* as seed parent, the results were more vigorous than those of the reciprocal cross. Although the hybrids are usually sterile, some of Parizek's produced a few seeds, and the second-generation (F_2) plants closely resembled their F_1 hybrid parents. Marguerite Norbo of Portland, Oregon, worked on this grex for a number of years. No further generations of this promising strain are known.

***Lewisia cotyledon* × *L. columbiana* var. *rupicola*.** Carl English first reported making this cross in the course of investigating *Lewisia columbiana* var. *rupicola*; he offered hybrid plants for sale around 1934. At about the same time, in Britain, spontaneous hybrids began to appear from lewisias raised from seed sent by English (first as *L. columbiana* var. *rosea*, later as *L. columbiana* var. *rupicola*). These hybrids had characteristics resembling those of whatever forms of *L. cotyledon* were growing near the *L. columbiana* var. *rupicola* parents. These hybrids differ from hybrids of the species' types mainly in having smaller rosettes and flowers with a smoky purplish cast.

Lewisia cotyledon var. ***howellii*** × ***L. columbiana*** var. ***rupicola.*** The mauve tint not common in the genus is often seen in this group. In the early 1940s Paul Giuseppi produced the hybrid 'Trevosia' from this cross. The name (spelled "trevosiana" in some early accounts) referred to his residence, Trevose, on the Suffolk coast. Stuart Boothman, whose Nightingale Nursery at Maidenhead cataloged this plant beginning around 1950, described it as "brightest of all, the coral of *howellii* wedded to the crimson-purple of *columbiana* [var.] *rosea*"—a sort of smoked-salmon color. 'Trevosia' won an Award of Merit at the Chelsea Flower Show on 25 May 1964, exhibited by Joe Elliott. Seed exchanges have included seed submitted under this name, but I know of no F_2 plants having been raised.

Though its origin is obscure, another longtime favorite is outwardly so similar to 'Trevosia' that it must be included here. 'George Henley', a 1950 foundling at Ingwersen's Birch Farm Nursery, was eventually named for the nursery foreman and introduced. Its rich green rosettes are wine-tinted underneath, and each leaf bears a few tiny teeth, suggesting *Lewisia cotyledon* var. *heckneri* ancestry. From May to fall, its many 6-inch (15-cm) stems bear a profusion of strawberry or brick-red flowers. This hybrid gained its Award of Merit when shown by Ingwersen on 22 May 1978.

Both 'George Henley' and 'Trevosia' have been frequent winners of the best-in-show Farrer and Forrest medals in the keen competitions of England and Scotland, respectively. Both conveniently produce plants with many small offset rosettes ("pups" to the enthusiast) for propagation.

Lewisia cotyledon × ***L. columbiana*** var. ***wallowensis.*** Fritz Kummert reported that this pair produced "notable results, a cross well worth repeating." The greatest promise is seen using the vigorous, small Idaho forms of *Lewisia columbiana* var. *wallowensis*, which cross, performed at Grand Ridge, has generated plants that resemble miniature versions of *L. cotyledon*, only 3 to 4 inches (7.5 to 10 cm) tall, but with many floriferous stalks, a fine color range, and great durability.

Lewisia cotyledon × ***L. oppositifolia.*** A reference to this combination appears in the records of the Royal Horticultural Society for 1923. A plant grown from a cross made in 1921 by a Mr. Gosden was referred to the scientific committee on 9 August 1922 and is described merely as "a deciduous plant with orange flower."

Although these two species grow in proximity to each other in Del Norte County, California, and Josephine County, Oregon, one inhabits ridges and cliffs while the other is a lowlander, flowering much earlier. They are not truly sympatric and have never been known to interbreed in the wild. The garden hybrid shows promise and is considered "no-

Ashwood Nurseries created this beauty by crossing *Lewisia oppositifolia* with an apricot hybrid of *L. cotyledon* JOHN MASSEY/PHILIP BAULK

table" by Fritz Kummert. Using the more compact *Lewisia oppositifolia* 'Richeyi' should be particularly promising, now that it has been reintroduced to gardens.

Lewisia cotyledon × *L. nevadensis, Lewisia cotyledon* × *L. pygmaea.* Crossing *Lewisia cotyledon* with either *L. nevadensis* or *L. pygmaea* or gives much the same results, none of them very durable. Especially beguiling are the very bright flowers obtained when the reddest forms of *L. cotyledon* are crossed with the rosiest *L. pygmaea*; the plants have jade rosettes with carved ruby blossoms. Jim Le Compte reported that an entrancing white form appeared in his New Zealand garden, "with a flower suggesting *rediviva*, a beautiful plant, but it left us."

Lewisia leeana × *L. columbiana* var. *rupicola.* Although he is not presently pursuing it, Burl Mostul of Rare Plant Research in Portland, Oregon, had success with this cross, which he accomplished quite easily. The resulting plants are vigorous growers.

Lewisia leeana × *L. cotyledon.* This is the only natural hybrid that occurs predictably in the wild—mostly in Siskiyou County, California, but sometimes in adjacent Oregon. The *Lewisia leeana* × *L. cotyledon* hybrids were first noted in the late 1920s by Mary White, who found plants on open ridges in the Siskiyous near the Illinois Basin of southern Oregon. She propagated her find and sent it to Carl Purdy, who distributed it through his nursery. In 1932 Purdy published this plant as a new species; its vegetatively propagated offspring should properly be referred to as *L.* ×*whiteae* 'Mary White' (Purdy) Mathew 1989. *Lewisia* ×*whiteae* is a grex that includes all hybrids of *L. leeana* and any form of *L. cotyledon*.

Lewisia ×*whiteae* is to be expected wherever *L. leeana* and *L. cotyledon* are sympatric. This hybrid has been found many times and in an amazing range of colors—white to yellow to apricot, mauve-lilac, pink, rose to deep cerise-crimson—and is usually solid-colored but sometimes

Burl Mostul of Rare Plant Research raised this interesting hybrid of *Lewisia pygmaea* and *L. cotyledon* BURL MOSTUL

The elegant progeny of *Lewisia leeana* and *L. columbiana* var. *rupicola* BURL
MOSTUL

striped. Its early misidentification as the rather similar *L. columbiana* led to the erroneous assumption that *L. columbiana* occurred in California.

Arthur Kruckeberg (1957) described these plants as "the quintessent hybrid among wildflowers," so perfectly intermediate are they in every way to their two parents, including habitat preference. Although wildflower enthusiasts had long recognized these plants as hybrids, this was not acknowledged by the scientific community until such hybrids were noted in the Marble Mountains of northern California (Tucker et al. 1964). Unpublished chromatographic investigations confirm this intermediate nature (Hohn 1975). Hohn found that these are also intermediate in the foliar flavonoids they produce. The hybrids bear little fertile pollen. Roger Raiche observed in a letter that except in color, these hybrids, apparently all of the F_1 generation, were much alike: "I never saw a trace of anything identifiable as a backcross, and if those do occur they are cryptic in appearance and rarer than the already rare F_1."

Some notable clones have been given cultivar names. Purdy's original introduction, *Lewisia* ×*whiteae* 'Mary White', is still in cultivation; it has salmon-rose flowers. *Lewisia* ×*whiteae* 'Margaret Williams' is a dark cerise-red found by a party that included J. M. Tucker in the Marble Mountains in 1964; it received an Award of Merit in England on 18 April 1967. 'Timmie Foster' (creamy yellow flowers with a rose center) was found in the wild and named by Lawrence Crocker and Boyd Kline, founders of the Siskiyou Rare Plant Nursery.

Lewisia enthusiasts can, of course, raise their own *Lewisia* ×*whiteae* hybrids without making the strenuous climb up to the Klamath haunts of the wild plants. Hohn grew some of her hand-pollinated seeds in carefully controlled conditions under glass. She utilized pollen brought in from wild plants and found, as had Kath Dryden, that the cross is next to impossible with *L. cotyledon* as the seed parent, although the reverse is easy. Hohn obtained no F_2 plants when she intercrossed the F_1 plants with one another or with *L. leeana*, but she got four seeds from crossing the F_1 with *L. cotyledon*. None germinated, however. Boyd Kline reported raising a plant of the F_2 generation in his Medford garden; it has also appeared at Ashwood Nurseries.

Lewisia longipetala × *L. cotyledon*. *Lewisia longipetala* has become rather famous in cultivation, not so much for its own merits as for its charming child 'Pinkie', raised by Ingwersen in England in the early 1960s and honored with the Award of Merit on 15 June 1965. This bewitching little plant inspired many other breeders to make the same cross, to good effect: we can now have versions of 'Pinkie' in almost every shade but blue! This cross is rated highly by Kummert and Parizek, although the latter was dismayed that the plants with the finest flowers produced few offsets for propagation.

'Pinkie' itself is a vigorous plant, making a cushion of almost grasslike, channeled, and pointed leaves, each about 2 inches (5 cm) long—a pleasing base for its myriad flowers. Each of many stalks bears as many

Will Ingwersen's famous *Lewisia* 'Pinkie' JOHN MASSEY/PHILIP BAULK

as six flowers; each flower has about eight petals, opening to about one inch (2.5 cm) across, colored persian rose. The color is subtle: on first opening the petals are suffused with rose over an opalescent buff ground, except at the clear butter-yellow base, and they seem to grow rosier as the buff pales during the day. The cup of sepals has prominent purple venation and glands; the anthers are cinnamon, and the pollen orange. 'Pinkie' proves the adage that good things come in small packages. With proper management it can flower continually through the summer.

In England, Philip Baulk has given us the pink 'Ashwood Pearl', and the Allens of M & R Nurseries introduced 'Matthew', a creamy-textured yellow-orange. A spontaneous hybrid, 'Ben Chace', was found at the Liverpool Botanic Gardens (the former Bulley estate) on the Wirral Peninsula in northwestern England. It has good clear pale pink flowers, 1.5 inches (3.5 cm) in diameter. Another seedling, 'Oxstalls Lane', differs from 'Pinkie' in having deep red anthers.

All these hybrids have the air of a delicate Sierran wildflower combined with the sturdiness of a Klamath cliff-maiden. A further attraction is the strong musky aroma bequeathed by *Lewisia longipetala* to all its offspring.

Ashwood Nurseries developed this pure yellow by crossing *Lewisia longipetala* with a yellow hybrid of *L. cotyledon* JOHN MASSEY/PHILIP BAULK

Lewisia rediviva × *L. brachycalyx.* Kath Dryden (Mathew 1989) is reported to have grown this hybrid. Such plants would not be expected to retain their leaves in summer, which they did.

Lewisia rediviva × *L. columbiana* var. ***columbiana.*** Although no plants have been observed form this cross, Hohn obtained seed by hand pollination in carefully controlled conditions.

Lewisia rediviva × *L. columbiana* var. *rupicola*. Parizek (1986) reported a single, curious plant from this combination (with *Lewisia rediviva* as the pollen parent). It grew into a cushion, reminiscent of an armeria, with several small flowers on short stalks, each about half the size of a *L. rediviva* flower and notable in that they retained the deep tint of *L. columbiana* var. *rupicola*. Cuttings, though freely available, rooted very poorly.

Lewisia rediviva × *L. cotyledon* var. *howellii*. *Lewisia* 'Weeks' Seedling', hybridized by A. G. Weeks, was given the Award of Merit on 1 July 1947. The published report notes merely that it was "said to have arisen from *L. rediviva* and *L. howellii* [*L. cotyledon* var. *howellii*]; appears valuable for it flowers over a long period." The accompanying photograph shows a distinguished and refined plant with plenty of narrow, plump foliage forming a cushion above which rise numerous stalks, each with several

An unnamed rosy apricot cross of *Lewisia cotyledon* and *L. longipetala* by Fritz Kummert FRITZ KUMMERT

flowers about 1.5 inches (3.5 cm) across; the dozen or so petals are pale pink with deeper pink markings from the center toward the slightly notched tips.

In the mid-1960s Joe Elliott repeated this cross and named the resulting plant *Lewisia* 'Redicot'. Fritz Kummert also had success with the cross, as did Ron Lutsko of California. All these hybrids held their foliage throughout the year. One of Kummert's unnamed plants has recently found favor as a satisfactory novelty in the Pacific Northwest. In England John Good named a plant of this derivation 'Pam', for his wife; it presents its strawberry-pink flowers all summer. Don Mann raised another, which Kath Dryden named 'Rawreth'; it has more of the bitterroot habit, combined with the flower of *Lewisia cotyledon* var. *howellii* 'Rose Splendour', its pollen parent. In California Steven Darington raised plants from crosses made both ways, using a large-flowered *L. cotyledon*; the resulting plants were quill-leaved, evergreen to semideciduous (depending on seed parent), long-lived, large flowered, and desirable. For some years, at White Salmon, Washington, Bruce Meyers grew a succession of hybrids in this grex.

Lewisia rediviva × *L. longipetala.* Kath Dryden has enjoyed both spontaneous and planned hybrids from this union, the marriage of a subalpine and a semidesert species. She has named a fine pink ('Roy Elliott') and a pair of whites ('Andrew' and 'Christine'). Tony Hall at Kew also succeeded with this exciting and unusual cross.

Lewisia stebbinsii × *L. cotyledon* var. *fimbriata.* Steven Darington is looking forward to flowering plants from this interesting cross, which resulted from using pollen of *Lewisia cotyledon* var. *fimbriata*.

Lewisia stebbinsii × *L. nevadensis.* This natural hybrid was collected by a party that included Nezzie Wade in June 1989, near the type location for *Lewisia stebbinsii*. Several individuals had an outward appearance sug-

Another fine hybrid from Ashwood Nurseries is this cross of a yellow hybrid of *Lewisia cotyledon* and a white-flowered *L. rediviva* JOHN MASSEY/PHILIP BAULK

Fritz Kummert accomplished this magnificent cross of *Lewisia rediviva* and *L. cotyledon* FRITZ KUMMERT

A natural hybrid of *Lewisia stebbinsii* and *L. nevadensis*, Mendocino County, California BURL MOSTUL

Kath Dryden crossed *Lewisia rediviva* × *L. cotyledon* with *L. nevadensis* × *L. brachycalyx* (*L. brachycalyx* parentage uncertain) to yield this lovely lewisia IAN CHRISTIE

gesting that they were hybrids with *L. nevadensis*. These plants had erect flowering stalks and foliage like neither of the putative parents—but curiously resembling that of *L. congdonii*. One of these specimens was deposited in the Humboldt State University herbarium in Arcata, California, by Wade; another, with lilac flowers, is retained living in my own collection for observation. Another such plant is on record at the California Academy of Sciences as having been found on nearby Leach Lake Mountain prior to the type collection of *L. stebbinsii*.

Lewisia triphylla × *L. nevadensis.* This natural hybrid was recorded in Lassen Volcanic National Park (Gillett et al. 1961). Wayne Roderick later found a representative at Castle Lake in eastern Siskiyou County, California.

CHAPTER SIX

Lewisias in Cultivation

MANY years after what was likely the first transplantation of *Lewisia cotyledon* from the wild to a garden, Clarice Paul Nye (1952) wrote:

> We were not looking for lewisias that summer day in 1890 when we went exploring up on Iron Creek Mountain. Being lately from the Plains states, we had never even heard of such a flower. We were pretty well toward the top when among the sedums and mosses the little star-shaped succulent caught all eyes; we succeeded in prying the rock away and got it out in good shape. Back home in Grants Pass, I made a little rock garden for it on the north side of the house, and when it bloomed the next year it was proclaimed by all visitors to be the nicest hen-and-chick they'd ever seen!

A History of Garden Lewisias—and People

Clarice Paul was a girl of ten or eleven at that time. She later married Nelson Nye and moved with him up the Rogue River to Prospect in Jackson County, Oregon, to raise their family, but she never lost her interest in wildflowers. She wrote about them and, in the late 1920s, started a small nursery. She propagated and disseminated a great variety of lewisias, many her own selections. Her business thrived and sustained the family through the Depression; she shipped plants throughout the world, even to the king of England. Her stony, raised nursery beds can still be seen under a high canopy of trees, and the family has kept up the old homestead even though the nursery closed with Mrs. Nye's death.

Lewisia cotyledon, with its great range of forms and colors, has always received the lion's share of attention from growers. This was stimulated by the enthusiasm of such great gardeners as Ellen Willmott, Max Leichtlin, and E. A. Bowles—and by the voluminous writings of Carl Purdy. Purdy focused on western American plants at a time when more excitement was being generated by the horticultural riches of the Himalayas and South Africa. From his large nursery east of Ukiah, California, Purdy shipped a great variety of plants, both native and exotic, making a specialty of lewisias from about 1910.

From 1914 to 1921 the Purdy catalogs offered much the same list of lewisias: *Lewisia columbiana*, *L. cotyledon*, *L. leeana*, *L. oppositifolia*, *L. rediviva*, and *L. tweedyi*. By 1935–1936 the list had expanded, organized into three groups according to growth habit and mode of cultivation, with detailed instructions for their management. The deciduous lewisias offered included *L. brachycalyx*, *L. nevadensis* (and the local variant billed as *L. bernardina*), *L. oppositifolia*, and *L. rediviva* (two forms, one a deep rose). The evergreen group, which Purdy called rockroses, comprised *L. columbiana*, *L. columbiana* var. *rupicola* (as *L. columbiana* var. *rosea*), *L. columbiana* 'Neeman's Variety', *L. leeana* (as the white *L. eastwoodiana*), and several varieties of *L. cotyledon* (*finchae*, *heckneri*, and *howellii* among them). *Lewisia tweedyi* by itself formed a third group. The 1939 catalog did not continue to list *L. eastwoodiana* and *L. columbiana* 'Neeman's Variety' but added *L. cotyledon* var. *fimbriata* (as *L. cotyledon* var. *heckneri* 'Elegans').

In the early twentieth century lewisias displayed at flower shows attracted quite a following in the northeastern United States. In the 1930s the catalog of Cronamere Nursery in Green Farms, Connecticut, offered a Carl Purdy selection alongside the Prairie Gem plants of Claude Barr. The amateur ordering *Lewisia leeana* or *L. rediviva* from this nursery must have been surprised at the package that arrived in the mail, since both plants were described in the nursery's catalog as "spiney."

Many of Purdy's hired collectors had an eye for exceptional individual plants. Two were the sisters-in-law Mary Finch and Mary White. Purdy honored both women in his names for unusual lewisias they had discovered; Mary Finch's plant has now been determined to be merely a form of *Lewisia cotyledon,* but Mary White's name survives in *L.* ×*whiteae.*

The third "lewisia Mary" of southwestern Oregon was Mary Byman of Canyonville in the South Umpqua Valley of Douglas County. Her finds were mainly forms of *Lewisia cotyledon* var. *howellii* from the cliffs of the Rogue River. In 1959 she received an award from the Oregon Federation of Garden Clubs of America in recognition of her developing the Byman Strain of *L. cotyledon,* raised principally from *L. cotyledon* var. *heckneri* and *L. cotyledon* var. *howellii* crossed with LePiniec's cotyledon hybrid 'Apricot Queen'. Among other species disseminated widely from Byman's garden were *L. oppositifolia* and the true *L. brachycalyx,* then new to cultivation. She was able to manage all these in the open garden, but she pronounced *L. tweedyi* "impermanent."

The Australian-born John Heckner, a government surveyor of Klamath Country, was another ardent amateur wildflower collector. His name is commemorated in the lewisia he discovered in the wild and propagated at his nursery in Brownsboro, *Lewisia cotyledon* var. *heckneri.* Heckner's concise catalog for 1933 offered *L. tweedyi, L. columbiana, L. columbiana* var. *rupicola* (as *L. columbiana* var. *rosea*), *L. oppositifolia, L. nevadensis, L. rediviva,* and six forms of *L. cotyledon,* along with exacting instructions for growing them. After the death of his wife, Heckner disappeared, suicidal. Years later his remains were found in the mountains he loved so well.

Although the name of Marcel LePiniec is not commemorated in that of any lewisia, it is closely associated with *Lewisia cotyledon* in the minds of veteran gardeners. Born in Brittany, as a boy Marcel was often charged with caring for the garden of his peripatetic father, a plant-loving captain of a channel-crossing boat. Among the plants Marcel remembered best were some lewisias his father grew from seed he had obtained at Kew. Much later Marcel had a long and successful career as a textile designer in

New York, with a plant hobby that grew into a second career when he founded Mayfair Nursery in New Jersey. His skill at designing rock gardens can still be seen at such East Coast estates as Winterthur in Delaware; his displays at flower shows won an almost embarrassing number of prizes, including sweepstakes awards.

In 1944 Marcel LePiniec sold Mayfair to travel west; he eventually settled in the Siskiyous, and soon he was selling plants again from a little roadside nursery in Phoenix, just outside Medford, Oregon. He became a keen plant explorer. He is credited with finding the Umpqua Valley form of *Kalmiopsis leachiana* and also the first white-flowered *Lewisia cotyledon* to be introduced into horticulture. He also increased and popularized the yellow-flowered *L. cotyledon* var. *howellii* 'Carroll Watson'.

Marcel's jovial humor endeared him to all, and his yarns, delivered in a rich and melodious Breton accent, caught everyone's imagination. (Some, indeed, remember him as an old windbag!) He never tired of recalling his boyhood in Brittany; nonetheless, his friends were surprised when, late in his life, he abruptly left Oregon and a wife of many years to return to Brittany and marry a childhood sweetheart. He was buried in the family graveyard just a few springs later.

Ed and Ethel Lohbrunner established a remarkable nursery in Victoria, British Columbia, around 1929, growing a burgeoning collection of alpine plants to which they added continuously through their own explorations of the West, the Continent, and Japan. Many other nursery growers trace their stocks to the Lohbrunners, particularly *Lewisia* ×*whiteae* (which they had originally received from Purdy). They also introduced a number of British cultivars to North America, including *L.* 'Trevosia' and *L. cotyledon* var. *howellii* 'Rose Splendour'.

Another devoted couple were Carl and Edith English—botanists, horticulturalists, collectors, and conservationists—who sold a few seeds and plants from their Seattle home. Edith English wrote a manual (published in 1929) of the plants of Mount Baker and was famous for her photography and her pastries; she also operated a summer nature school and youth camp. Carl English was for forty years a gardener at the Hiram Chittenden Government Locks in Seattle; the remarkable garden he developed there is now his memorial. Among their discoveries were *Claytonia nivalis* and *Lewisia columbiana* var. *rupicola*; Carl English published both in 1932 and named the hybrid of *L. columbiana* var. *columbiana* and *L. columbiana* var. *rupicola* that he had raised *L.* ×*edithae*, for his wife.

Charles Thurman of Spokane County in eastern Washington was another wildflower propagator, best known for his great success with *Lewisia tweedyi*. His catalog passed along his knowledge about growing this species, wisdom repeated in both editions of Elliott's monograph and in these pages. Charley installed a meandering basalt drywall in Spokane's Manito Park; it was for years an inspiration to all gardeners, especially for its crowning display of apricot *L. tweedyi*, which flourished just below the capping slabs in spite of summer overhead watering to roses and nearby lawns.

Dorothy King Young enjoyed creating and tending several gardens on the California coast, all featuring lewisias. In particular, through her writing, she contributed greatly to popularizing the wildflowers of the redwood belt, referring to this region's wild variant of *Lewisia cotyledon* as cliff-maidens, which name she offered as a translation of the Klamath Indian nation's word for the plant. In 1969 botanists from around the world who had come to Seattle to attend the Eleventh International Botanical Congress traveled south to San Francisco. En route, they visited the Youngs' garden in Mendocino County, "to see a typical American backyard garden." They were amazed by the acres overflowing with native wildflowers—none more striking than the lewisias billowing out of hollow-log planters, like dugout canoes filled with flowers.

Many others had a hand, or trowel, in the lewisia saga. Lawrence Crocker and Boyd Kline established the Siskiyou Rare Plant Nursery in Medford in 1963. Crocker had learned the plants of the Siskiyous with the help of John Heckner, while Kline earlier had gone plant-hunting with Marcel LePiniec. The two of them also visited Clarice Nye and Mary

Byman. It was a fitting tribute when Crocker and Kline became the first recipients of the North American Rock Garden Society's LePiniec Award, given to persons responsible for introducing and popularizing North American plants among gardeners. Their nursery is now owned by Baldassare Mineo, whose 1998 catalog offered five *Lewisia* taxa, including *Lewisia brachycalyx*, and two hybrid cultivars.

Gardeners everywhere, especially in England, benefited from the shared knowledge and seeds of Margaret Williams of Sparks, Nevada. With her family and a hardy band of wildflower enthusiasts—the nucleus of the Northern Nevada Native Plant Society—she traveled throughout the plant hot spots of the West, recording her observations in many articles. Although lewisias were not too happy in her Nevada garden, set into a beautiful but blazing hot red-rock exposure, she enjoyed them in the wild and helped others to understand their needs.

From Kirkland, Washington, near Seattle, George Schenk and his Wild Garden Nursery offered a broad selection of lewisias through the mail from 1960 to 1980. His first catalog included *Lewisia columbiana*, *L. columbiana* var. *rupicola*, *L. cotyledon* f. *alba*, *L. cotyledon* var. *howellii*, *L. cotyledon* var. *purdyi*, *L.* 'Wheatley's Variety' (*L. cotyledon* × *L. columbiana*), *L.* ×*edithae*, *L. leeana*, *L. nevadensis*, and *L. oppositifolia*. Unfortunately this fascinating nursery closed when Schenk retired, but Robert Putnam, another Seattle-area nurseryman, sold plants only locally into the 1980s. He once offered *Lewisia maguirei* as well as several of Janet Hohn's collections. Upon Putnam's death, his plants passed to Phil Pearson and Steve Doonan of Grand Ridge Nursery.

Among the Californians who have enriched horticulture with their knowledge of lewisias are staff members, present and past, of the University of California Botanical Garden in Berkeley. Doyen of California seed collectors, the tireless Wayne Roderick is just as well known for his many years of introducing visitors to California's plants in the wild. Roger Raiche followed in this tradition and established a remarkably successful private garden; he has lately retired to a business of landscape design.

While at Berkeley, Sean Hogan specialized in lewisias and is coauthor of the section on *Lewisia* for the forthcoming *Flora of North America*, prepared under the auspices of the Missouri Botanical Garden; he has recently returned to Portland, Oregon, to start a nursery.

How to Grow Lewisias

"From being miffy, troublesome plants, the lewisias have become so much at home they sow themselves everywhere as common weeds when given suitable soil conditions," wrote Charles Musgrave in the report of the First Rock Garden Conference, held in England in 1936.

This should not be taken to imply that one can succeed with lewisias without even trying. Musgrave's comments notwithstanding, other authors' reservations about them are all too true. They are exacting plants—some, to be sure, less than others—both in nature and in cultivation. The suggestions that follow are not dogma; as with any plant, it is necessary to understand the climatic and soil conditions present and adjust one's gardening techniques accordingly.

Lewisias are as easy to grow as sedums when their precise but simple needs are satisfied. These needs involve moisture, drainage, light, and shelter from blisteringly hot heat. Lewisias prosper in cool conditions: even those that grow in the dry wastelands of the West enjoy cool microclimates in their root-runs during their growth period. The gardener who lives in a region of low rainfall, low humidity, and cool nights may succeed in growing lewisias without half trying. For others, especially in hot, humid areas, they may remain a tantalizing challenge, although pot culture is possible anywhere.

Water is undoubtedly the most critical factor in the cultivation of these plants. First let us consider lewisias that want water only during the spring growth period. They dry off as their flowering is completed, and they have only mere traces of soil moisture for the rest of the summer; they enjoy a cool position, however. These must be kept on the dry side in all seasons except spring, but never parched bone-dry; this is true even for

Selections and hybrids of *Lewisia cotyledon* massed at Burl Mostul's Rare Plant Research nursery, refuting the common wisdom that lewisias are "difficult"!
BURL MOSTUL

the bitterroot and the other two species of section *Lewisia*. In the garden, it is safest to plant these in a raised bed of gritty soil retained by surface stones, or on a rather steep slope where the soil is held in place by a good admixture of small stones, which also reduces soil erosion and provides a cool root-run. These beds should slope away from the angle of the summer sun; in the Northern Hemisphere, a north or northeast exposure is preferable, or northwest if it is lightly shaded in the afternoon.

The perfect rock garden habitat for lewisias: a well-drained soil retained by rocks, which provide a cool root-run BURL MOSTUL

Species of section *Pygmaea* grow in the wild where moisture persists well into the summer, at least until their seeds are ripening. They sometimes associate with heath climax vegetation near cool mountain forests, including such genera as *Vaccinium* and *Pyrola*. They enter dormancy late in the season. Unfortunately, these lewisias are the least showy, with small, usually pallid flowers; they can, however, present a charming effect when grown in large numbers, as we often see them in moist mountain meadows. Deeper colors—pink, rose, or ruby-crimson in *Lewisia pygmaea*—can be sought out and perpetuated from seed. The odd little *L. triphylla* is frequently found with members of this section, and it appreciates the same conditions in the garden. Neither the species of section *Pygmaea* nor *L. triphylla* will flower without experiencing low temperatures in winter.

The evergreen plants of section *Cotyledon* and *Lewisia tweedyi* are easier to cope with, perhaps because the leaves are present all year long as a guide to what is going on with the plant. Many of these lewisias are valuable for their foliage rosettes alone, especially the ruffled leather of *L. cotyledon* var. *howellii* and the toothed varieties, *L. cotyledon* var. *fimbriata* and *L. cotyledon* var. *heckneri*. *Lewisia cantelovii* and *L. serrata* are primarily foliage plants, with less than riveting flowers. This is also true of the robust *L. congdonii*, although it is only semideciduous; given supplementary water in summer to keep it cool, it persists in both leaf and flowering.

In the open garden, it is imperative to place all lewisias where they will be high and dry, as well as cool. It is fascinating to note the exposures they favor in the wild. Even when associated with shade-casting trees and shrubs, as they commonly are, the lewisias grow far enough from the taller plants that they experience neither dense shade nor dripping water. Even though some can be found in moss that is saturated in spring, they are not being dripped on from above; and though the soil is certainly full of water, that water is moving, not stagnant.

The substrate of most lewisias in the wild is a combination of humus with the detritus of rock slides and exfoliating cliffs. This soil is light and porous: it retains a certain necessary amount of moisture, but the excess drains away instantly. In early spring, when their growth is at its peak, lewisias are far more moisture-tolerant than at any other time. Most species seem to prefer soil that is neutral to slightly acid, although they can be seen occasionally on limestone substrates. Many even prosper on serpentine outcrops, where the mineral content is toxic to many other plants.

There are as many recipes for the ideal soil for growing lewisias in the garden as there are growers. The soil should begin with a good loam with an airy, earthy smell. This should be opened up with plenty of coarse grit—not fine sand, which will pack tightly. If it is available, crushed pumice is the ideal amendment. A mulch of stone chips is essential for keeping the foliage dry and clean and checking erosion.

Lewisias should never suffer the midday heat. Orient them to the north on a slope, if possible; if not, the shade of suitably distant trees, shrubs, or structures helps to maintain the dry yet cool conditions they crave. The north side of an east-west wall is ideal. Of the evergreen species, only *Lewisia leeana, L. columbiana,* and some forms of *L. cotyledon,* with their much reduced leaf surfaces, tolerate much summer sun. The deciduous species escape the summer heat by estivating; they go underground.

Although lewisias can endure much deprivation, starved plants cannot bear comparison to well-fed ones, such as those Joan Means grows in her Massachusetts garden in "rich and watered soil, laced with old cow manure" (but she provides very sharp drainage and midday shade). Even the semidesert soils inhabited by such species as *Lewisia brachycalyx* and *L. rediviva* are nutrient-rich because they have never been subject to leaching by rainfall.

A common dictum is that lewisias detest watering. Of course they must have water: they simply do not enjoy being wet. The amount of water given should never be great, and watering should be done only when both leaves and mulch can dry off rapidly. Water should never be applied when the plant is limp from desiccation; first, cool it by shading it, and then revive it by supplying water a little bit at a time, until the leaves regain their healthy plumpness. If this procedure is not followed, rot is likely to result.

One technique for growing lewisias in areas of summer rainfall is to keep them in a covered frame, such as a bulb frame. In fact, lewisias and small bulbs make a very satisfactory combination. The frame can be set into a slope or built up as a covered raised bed, with rockwork added. Plant it just as you would a raised scree bed, with the lewisias in cool clefts and the bulbs tucked among them. These companion plants should be only smallish subjects, such as *Crocus*, lest they cast a detrimental shadow.

Lewisias survive through special adaptations that enable them to weather severe drought. But neither in the wild nor in cultivation are they sociable plants. Where conditions allow shrubs or rank annual weeds to invade, the lewisias retreat. This teaches us to allow them plenty of room in the garden, with no competitive mat-forming subjects or overhanging shrubs in close proximity. In nature, sedums, rock ferns, selaginellas, and small penstemons coexist happily with lewisias, but these must be restrained so that they do not jostle, elbow, or otherwise annoy their companions.

One last fundamental truth is that all lewisias are inherently cold-hardy. That is, they are capable of escaping damage from freezing where they occur naturally. Most, however, can be damaged to some degree if exposed to sudden cold when they are in full spring growth. Therefore, some shelter—even a couple of layers of newspaper—can temper the cold by several degrees and preserve the plant. A frozen plant should not be thawed with applied heat. Shelter it from sudden warmth, even from the sun. A newspaper or bath towel, held in place against the wind, can ease the shocking transition between freezing and thawing in the open garden.

Naturally, plants growing vigorously in ideal conditions prove more tolerant of adversity. The gardener who has lost a plant in cold weather must consider all the variables when performing the autopsy: was it too wet, too dry, too sunny, too shady, or none of the above? Was there evidence of disease?

No one ever counseled on lewisia culture more succinctly than Marcel

LePiniec (1964). His six rules apply equally to cultivation in the garden or in containers:

1. Very good drainage is essential.
2. A lean gritty soil should be subacid to neutral (pH 6–7).
3. Use no manures, though a feeding (such as liquid fish emulsion) may be applied in spring as soon as plants have lost their winter flabbiness. [This was offered before the advent of pelletized fertilizer.]
4. Site plants away from all midday heat, preferably facing north or northwest.
5. Site plants away from all drips, such as from trees.
6. Be especially watchful for orange fungus, removing even the tiniest spot of it on leaves or rootstock; pull old spent leaves cleanly away [better yet, trim them to short stalks, which will soon drop away]; dust open wounds with a fungicide immediately.

Skilled growers manage to maintain lewisias outdoors in New England, Norway, and even in Iceland. Attention to these cultural requirements should make them accessible to most careful gardeners, wherever they live.

Lewisias in Containers

The portability of container plants is an obvious advantage. They can be moved about to suit the convenience of the gardener, displayed in an otherwise color-starved garden, or even—briefly—enliven the indoors. They can be given to friends or taken to shows. They can be removed to warmer or cooler or drier positions, as the weather dictates.

In addition to all this, lewisias are easiest to grow in containers. Few rock garden plants lend themselves so well to this form of cultivation. Lewisias flourish best when grown in any sort of container—pot, pan, bowl, drilled rock, hollow log, drilled hubcap. Thus they are favored alpine house subjects, even though most are not true alpines in the wild;

yet they seem to remember a colder ancestral time, and most occur only where snow and frost are part of the annual cycle.

The critical factor in container growing is total control of the environment: light, water, temperature, humidity, and soil. This is said to sharpen the gardener's wits. Fortunately, lewisias are not quite as exacting as many other plants; however, container-grown plants should be examined carefully and frequently to note the onset of fungal diseases, which can kill a plant quickly.

From the earliest days of lewisia cultivation, gardeners have passed on advice that can be summed up in three words: drainage, drainage, drainage. Like all plants, lewisias must have water to grow, but they cannot cope with an excessive amount of it. Norm Deno would abolish the word! When moisture leaves the soil, air replaces it, and this aeration is particularly critical for lewisias. In no case should mature plants of the deciduous species have water following their flowering period in summer; seedlings, however, tend to tolerate more summer water in their first year, but not thereafter.

Even lewisias that do not actually estivate in summer are not actively growing at this time; they must be kept cool, or they may simply burn out. These plants can endure extreme desiccation as long as their roots remain cool. More plants are lost from well-intended watering in summer, when they are most vulnerable to fungal attack, than from any other cause.

A frazzled-looking plant in a container can be moved to a cooler place to recover; if the container is large and heavy, a shade of lath or other material can be erected above it. Moist-

Most lewisias excel in containers given the proper regimen; this *Lewisia brachycalyx* is no exception SEAN HOGAN

ened burlap is excellent; the evaporation of the water adds a cooling effect. Misting can be an aid to cooling, but it must be carefully done: just direct a fine spray quickly past the plant, repeating this again and again, but not so often that the foliage becomes wet.

With the arrival of cooler weather in fall, we note a quiet stirring in the plants. Some of the deciduous ones show tiny points of green, and the evergreen rosettes develop a fresher color in the centers. This is the signal to begin giving water. The first waterings should be only a trace, a promise. Clay pots may be dipped—but never stood—in water. They can become quite dry before this process is repeated, but the soil need not shrivel between waterings.

During the winter the atmosphere where the pots are kept should be buoyant, even breezy. There must be good light, even direct sunshine. If the pots are plunged in sand, they will not dry out too thoroughly. A modicum of moisture is the goal.

With spring warmth, the leaves begin to elongate, and the flower buds of many species (including *Lewisia tweedyi*, which sets buds in the fall) start enlarging. This is the signal to give more water. During this rapid growth period the plants can handle all the water they can get, as long as it is not stagnant. Now is the time to apply fertilizer very lightly. A very dilute liquid feeding can be given frequently; pelleted slow-release fertilizer is an excellent alternative.

The soil mix or compost for container-grown lewisias can consist of one-half to two-thirds chippings (fine crushed rock with most of the dust washed away) and coarse sharp sand or crushed pumice; the remainder will consist of humus-rich loam. It is traditionally recommended that the lower part of the container be filled with crocking of broken clay pots or coarse rock chips and the top dressed with gravel or stone chips. Most growers no longer consider crocking necessary: it is thought actually to inhibit drainage. A fine mesh screen at the bottom of the pot will deter cutworms and other pests from entering.

These recommendations apply to cultivation in clay pots, the traditional container. Plastic pots can be used, but extra care must then be given to providing drainage and maintaining the correct moisture level. Valuable specimen plants can be double-potted, or planted in a clay pot inside another, larger one; the space between the pots is filled with sand, and water is added only to the sand, thoroughly but not too often.

Climatic differences dictate a slightly different approach to growing lewisias in Britain and elsewhere. In the English Midlands, Ashwood Nurseries maintains its plants in well-ventilated greenhouses to avoid the precipitation that can fall any month of the year, even though the total precipitation is only about 25 inches (63 cm) annually. Evergreen lewisias are kept in active growth March through November by meticulous moisture control, while deciduous sorts are allowed to dry off into dormancy at the end of flowering. The specific period of dormancy varies from species to species, with many of section *Pygmaea* continuing growth until halted by lowering temperatures.

Philip Baulk oversees both plant production and selective breeding of the Ashwood color strains of *Lewisia cotyledon*. His article "My Lewisia Year" provides a detailed account of procedures followed in the nursery, from seed-sowing, pricking out, growing on, and flowering to selection, pollination, seed harvest, storage, and planting again—all one needs to know about growing these lewisias in Britain (Baulk 1988).

Pests and Diseases

A menagerie of fauna is attracted to lewisias. Deer often browse the succulent rosettes, as do bears. Rodents nibble the foliage and burrow after the starchy rootstocks. Anchoring plants in stone-filled crevices is the safest way to protect them from such attacks.

Lewisias can also host root-mining maggots, the larvae of the carrot fly (*Psila rosae*, normally a pest of umbellifers) or of the carnation fly (*Delia cardui, D. brunnescens*). The maggots create superficial mines in the caudex and rootstock, sometimes going into the cortex. The adult fly deposits its eggs, which hatch into larvae that feed on the tissue—apparently thinking they are enjoying some familiar vegetable. The result is not only disfiguring, it leaves the damaged tissue vulnerable to fungus infection. This is reported to be a particular nuisance with *Lewisia tweedyi*, although other species may be similarly threatened.

Cutworms and slugs are present in most gardens, and spraying or baiting is advised. In the alpine house, whiteflies and aphids can be a serious annoyance, as can sowbugs, mealybugs, and even earthworms, but G. H. Berry (1952) reported that spring spraying for aphids with a nicotine compound totally arrested all development of flower buds on *Lewisia tweedyi*. "Lewisias dislike chemicals" is indeed a frequent but vague complaint, and lewisias are sensitive to chemical substances as a rule. But a systemic granular insecticide is considered a safe treatment and the best control for most insects attacking container plants, though it is not guaranteed for lewisias.

Two diseases are of particular concern in lewisias: damping off of seedlings, and the dreaded orange fungus. The best way to avoid damping off is to grow the seedlings outdoors in cool, breezy conditions. If they must be grown indoors, try the surface sterilization method recommended by Norman Deno (in his self-published—most recently in 1996—*Seed Germination: Theory and Practice*): pour a little boiling water over the top of the seed pot just before sowing the seed.

The orange fungus disease strikes in high summer, turning a sturdy plant into a stinking mass of decay in short order. The organism responsible is probably a species of *Botrytis*. Prevention consists of keeping plant surfaces dry and providing free drainage and air circulation. Dusting with a fungicide is recommended during warm, wet weather.

The succulent leaves of lewisias can be pocked by hailstones to the extent that the leaf surface is broken, disfiguring the plant or, worse, allowing fungi to enter the tissue. In the evergreen sorts, where the foliage persists for some time, the threat of hailstones is an ongoing annoyance; a high cover of shade cloth will deflect the hailstones while simultaneously providing relief from intense sunshine.

Seed Propagation

Clarice Nye (1952) was confident from the beginning that lewisias could easily be raised from seed. She prescribed perfect drainage and an acid soil of well-rotted conifer needles and rock chips, with more chips as a mulch. The seeds, planted in fall, germinated in her nursery in very early spring. They required very little watering—just enough so that the clay pot felt cool. "Seedlings are fat little fellows," she warned, "and the frost lifts them out, so they must be carefully watched and protected until roots are developed enough to hold."

Writers reporting on germination seem to agree that it can be sporadic. It is now thought that most portulacad seeds contain natural substances that inhibit germination. These compounds must degrade over time, which mechanism allows the seed to survive the hostile winter intact, germinating only in spring when conditions are optimal for the seedling's survival. It is therefore advisable to provide a period of moist chilling after the seed is sown, as Nye did by sowing her seed only in fall in the open. In warmer areas, or if planting must be delayed until spring, moist chilling for three weeks at 38°F (3°C) produces satisfactory germination. Seed that is planted late and not chilled may lie dormant for a year, then startle the grower with 100 percent germination overnight. It is best to keep the surface of the seed pot or flat quite dry, watering it from below when moisture is deemed necessary.

Norman Deno, who has conducted several examinations of lewisia germination, recommends, in addition to the outdoor treatment already described, soaking the seeds in a solution of gibberellic acid before sowing. This GA-3 treatment has recently enjoyed a considerable vogue among alpine growers, but the resulting seedlings, though numerous, tend to be etiolated and weak. Deno has noted that garden seed of *Lewisia tweedyi* in particular was poorly set and low in viability using that method.

Once new seedlings have ceased to emerge, what do we do next? If the seedlings are not crowded, it is well to leave them undisturbed. Otherwise, they may be transplanted to individual pots or moved into flats, spaced well apart. Transplanting, however, may induce dormancy, and the transplanted seedlings may become overly sensitive to water for the rest of the season.

If you are growing lewisias intended for the open garden, it is good to plant at least a portion of them into their permanent site while they are very small. As long as they are not too hot, such tiny seedlings may surprise you with their vigor and longevity, besting plants moved into the garden when they were much larger.

Kept sufficiently uncrowded, seedlings need not be fertilized. Crowded plants, however, lose vigor in the competition for nutrients, and they never regain their strength. In such cases, a dilute feeding with a low-nitrogen fertilizer may be beneficial. In general, however, it is wise to keep the seedlings growing heartily through their first summer without force-feeding them, lest they become lush and prone to decay. Indeed, as with so many other winter growers, they can often do without summer dormancy their first year, especially if kept cool.

Propagation by Cutting

How old is the oldest known lewisia plant? No one has ever determined, but some specimens in the wild appear to be very old. Garden plants of *Lewisia cotyledon* are known to have thrived at least forty years. In the wild, very old, ropy, mostly decayed plants of *L. tweedyi* are surely much older; they sometimes make colonies, with the living ends rooting individually while the old caudex decays. Thus lewisias increase naturally from what are essentially cuttings.

Propagation by cutting off and rooting the small offset rosettes (or pups) has long been a way of increasing many different lewisias. Presumably all species could be handled in this way. Cuttings are, however, most useful as a means of increasing sterile hybrids or special selections. This is also an emergency method of salvaging a plant that has lost its caudex to rot: the rosettes into which the rot has not yet progressed are cut off, cleaned, dried briefly, and treated with a little sulfur or a fungicide before being set into a medium to reroot (Hogan 1990).

Cuttings are best taken in early spring, when a long rooting season can be anticipated, although they can be successful at any time of year. Preparation for commercial production of evergreen lewisias from cuttings begins in summer, when the lower leaves are stripped away. A tiny sprout then emerges in the axil where each leaf has been removed. In the flush of the next spring's growth, these propagules are cut away and left until the wound has dried before being inserted in the rooting medium. Rooting hormones may contribute to a successful outcome, particularly if the compound includes a fungicide.

The rooting medium must be very free-draining and airy. Some growers use a mixture of sand, peat, and perlite; others prefer pure crushed pumice. The container should be enclosed, to admit plenty of light but to prevent desiccation. The medium should be just moist, not too wet. A small box or flat, or a large clay pot, can be set over a shallow container filled with gravel and water to maintain this buoyant condition. The cuttings should never be exposed to direct sun—only light, not heat, is essential. Rooting can be quite slow or very fast, depending on the season and the vigor of the material. The new plants should be potted up when a good brush of roots has formed but before the roots become inconveniently stringy.

Propagation by leaf cuttings has been mentioned in the gardening literature. A leaf with a "heel" (a bit of stalk tissue) is carefully treated in the manner just described for pups. But this is a slow process and not one to be encouraged other than as a last resort, when a plant produces no off-sets. Leaf cuttings sometimes produce roots for several years, during which the original leaf grows quite plump, but no plant is formed; obviously, such leaves were taken without axillary growth buds.

Micropropagation

Micropropagation, or tissue culture, presents a new frontier in lewisia growing. Tissue culture is now used to produce vast quantities of clones from choice selections of popular garden plants such as lilies. This is a laboratory procedure that generates plants in vitro (in test tubes under aseptic conditions) from tiny portions of plant tissue—most commonly from the meristem tips (growing points) of apical or axial growth buds with primordial photosynthetic leaves attached.

In evergreen rosulate lewisias, this tissue is concealed within the growing point centering each leaf rosette; with other lewisias this tissue is subterranean, at the apex of the rootstock. Attempts to micropropagate lewisias are still highly experimental, and while some encouraging successes have been achieved, the overall results are inconsistent (Walkey 1991).

Burl Mostul's work in tissue culture of lewisias has dramatically improved since he began using some of the recently developed bacterial and fungal suppressants with his media. "The biggest difficulty with *Lewisia* has been getting explants free from contamination. With these new inhibitors, tissue culture has been much easier" (pers. comm. 1998). He has been working on micropropagating one sterile cross, *Lewisia cotyledon* × *L. longipetala*, which blooms at least four times or more during the growing season and has many more flowers than either species produces singly. He believes this attractive cross holds great promise.

Exhibiting Lewisias

Gardeners in North America, especially in the West, are not so deeply involved in the competitive side of growing plants as are those abroad, particularly in Britain. There the award system of the Royal Horticultural

Society, by focusing attention on meritorious plants, generates considerable friendly rivalry—as well as a few raised hackles and bruised egos. Exhibiting plants requires the production of a perfection as fleeting as it is impressive. No matter how good a specimen appears at the moment, in a few years it may be difficult to recall just how good it was.

Over the years the genus *Lewisia* has garnered its fair share of honors, both at the regular shows of the Royal Horticultural Society and Alpine Garden Society and at the annual Chelsea extravaganza . The most coveted awards are the First Class Certificate (F.C.C.) and Award of Merit (A.M.); the Preliminary Commendation (P.C.) is given to newly introduced plants that show exceptional promise. There are also best-in-show medals, those in England named in honor of the alpine-plant expert Reginald Farrer, and those in Scotland for the plant explorer George Forrest. A cultural commendation may recognize the skill of the exhibitor in bringing to near perfection a subject not easy in cultivation. On occasion, silver or gold medals honor significant exhibits reflecting both the skill of the grower and the unique quality of the plants shown.

Three lewisias have been awarded the First Class Certificate: *Lewisia rediviva*, exhibited by the Messrs. Backhouse in 1873; *Lewisia cotyledon* f. *alba* 'Kathy Kline', shown by Kath Dryden in 1972; and *Lewisia* 'George Henley' (which also won an Award of Merit in 1978) in 1997, exhibited by Dr. Cyril Lafong. The Award of Merit has been granted over the years by the Royal Horticultural Society to the following lewisias:

1901   *Lewisia tweedyi*

1911   *Lewisia cotyledon*

1912   *Lewisia cotyledon* var. *howellii*

1915   *Lewisia columbiana*

1927   *Lewisia rediviva* 'Winifred Herdman'

1929   *Lewisia pygmaea*

1932   *Lewisia cotyledon* var. *heckneri*

1938   *Lewisia brachycalyx*

1947   *Lewisia* 'Weeks' Seedling'
1951   *Lewisia cotyledon* var. *howellii* 'Weald Rose'
1959   *Lewisia tweedyi* 'Rosea'
1964   *Lewisia* 'Trevosia'
1965   *Lewisia cotyledon* var. *howellii* 'Rose Splendour'
         Lewisia 'Pinkie'
1967   *Lewisia* ×*whiteae* 'Margaret Williams'
1970   *Lewisia oppositifolia*
1972   *Lewisia cotyledon* f. *alba* 'Monsieur LePiniec'
         Lewisia 'Phyllellia'
1974   *Lewisia cotyledon* var. *howellii* 'Carroll Watson'
1976   *Lewisia rediviva* 'Jolon'
1978   *Lewisia tweedyi* 'Alba'

A Note on Conservation

Of the varied assemblage of fauna that affects the well-being of lewisias, humans have had the most destructive effect. Native Americans gathered the bitterroot for sustenance; later Americans dug the plants from the wild to sell to gardeners. As lewisias are so easy to grow from seed, to gather anything but seed from the wild, or at the most a few cuttings, is thoughtless indeed.

Even those in high places are not free of guilt. When we encounter the name of Theodore Roezl we usually remember the lily named in his honor, yet a single shipment of his southwestern bulb collections (mostly lily bulbs) dispatched to the European market weighed in at 10 tons (9 metric tons). E. H. Wilson was justly proud of introducing *Lilium regale*, easily grown from seed, but he did not regret having gathered several thousand of its bulbs from the wild—and he was all but canonized for the accomplishment. Many collectors were guilty of gathering for profit in the past, but Carl Purdy, who has been criticized of late, also maintained a nursery in which he propagated and increased his selections.

Still, more precious wild plants have been destroyed by loss of habitat than by all the effects of all the collectors combined. (Wayne Roderick was recently elated by a season that featured tremendous flowering among *Calochortus* in the wild, possibly attributable to improved land management practices, coupled with benign weather after a series of drought years.) In short, the collection of seed in the wild has little impact on most populations because very few of the seeds dispersed under natural conditions ever produce plants. In cultivation, by contrast, a high proportion can be induced to germinate and grow to adulthood. Is it not time to forgive and forget the transgressions of past times, when nature was regarded as an infinitely self-renewing force?

Selected Bibliography

Agassiz, Louis. 1877. *Geological Sketches.* Boston: James R. Osgood.

Barr, Claude A. 1983. *Jewels of the Plains.* Minneapolis: University of Minnesota Press.

Baulk, Philip. 1988. My lewisia year. *Quarterly Bulletin of the Alpine Garden Society* 56 (3): 243.

Berry, G. H. 1952. *Lewisia tweedyi. Quarterly Bulletin of the Alpine Garden Society* 20 (2): 163.

Brandegee, Mary Katharine. 1894. Studies in Portulacaceae. *Proceedings of the California Academy of Sciences* 2 (4): 86–91.

Carolin, Roger C. 1987. A review of the family Portulacaceae. *Australian Journal of Botany* 35: 383–412.

Clay, Sampson. 1937. *The Present-Day Rock Garden.* London: T. C. & E. C. Jack, Ltd. Reprinted 1976 (Little Compton, R.I.: Theophrastus Publishers).

Daubenmire, Rexford. 1975. An ecological life-history of *Lewisia rediviva* (Portulacaceae). *Syesis* 8:9–23.

Dempster, Lauramay T. 1990. A new name combination in *Lewisia* (Portulacaceae) *Phytologia* 68 (3): 169–170.

———. 1993. *Lewisia.* In *The Jepson Manual: Higher Plants of California.* Ed. James C. Hickman. Berkeley and Los Angeles: University of California Press.

———. 1996. A new subspecies of *Lewisia* (Portulacaceae) in California. *Madroño* 43 (3): 415–416.

DeSanto, Jerry. 1993. *Bitterroot.* Babb, Mont.: Lere Press.

———. 1998. A rare color variation in three species of *Lewisia*. *Rock Garden Quarterly* 56 (2): 142.

Elliott, Roy C. 1966. *The Genus Lewisia.* London: Alpine Garden Society. 2d ed. 1978; originally published 1966 in the *Quarterly Bulletin of the Alpine Garden Society* 34:1–76.

Ferlatte, William J. 1974. *A Flora of the Trinity Alps of Northern California.* Berkeley: University of California Press.

Ferris, Roxanna S. 1944. *Lewisia.* In *Illustrated Flora of the Pacific States.* Vol. 2. Ed. LeRoy Abrams. Stanford, Calif.: Stanford University Press.

Fosberg, Francis. 1942. Notes on North American plants, part 2. *American Midland Naturalist* 27 (1): 253–258.

Gabrielson, Ira N. 1932. *Western American Alpines.* New York: Macmillan.

Gankin, R. W., and W. R. Hildreth. 1968. A new species of *Lewisia* from Mendocino County, California. *Four Seasons* 2:12–14.

Gillett, G. W., J. T. Howell, and H. Leschke. 1961. A flora of Lassen Volcanic National Park, California. *Wasmann Journal of Biology* 19:1–185.

Gray, Asa. 1887. Contributions to American botany 1. Revisions of some polypetalous genera and orders precursory to the *Synoptical Flora of North America. Proceedings of the American Academy of Arts and Sciences* 22:270–306.

Heckard, L. R., and G. L. Stebbins. 1974. A new *Lewisia* (Portulacaceae) from the Sierra Nevada of California. *Brittonia* 26:305–308.

Hershkovitz, Mark A. 1990. Nomenclatural changes in Portulacaceae. *Phytologia* 68 (4): 267–270.

Hitchcock, C. Leo. 1964. *Synoptic Flora of the Pacific Northwest.* Seattle: University of Washington Press.

Hogan, Sean. 1990. Lewisias in cultivation. *Bulletin of the American*

Rock Garden Society 48 (1): 47–52. Reprinted 1996 in *Rock Garden Plants of North America* (Portland, Ore.: Timber Press).

Hohn, Janet E. 1975. Biosystematic studies of the genus *Lewisia*, section *Cotyledon* (Portulacaceae). Ph.D. diss., University of Washington.

Holmgren, Arthur H. 1954. A new lewisia from Nevada. *Leaflets of Western Botany* 7 (6): 135–137.

———. 1955. Portulacaceae of Nevada. *Contributions towards a Flora of Nevada* 36:1–18.

Hooker, W. J., and G. A. W. Arnott. 1839. Lewisiaceae. In *The Botany of Captain Beechey's Voyage; California Supplement.* London: Henry G. Bohm.

Howell, Thomas Jefferson. 1893. A rearrangement of the American Portula[ca]ceae. *Erythea* 1:29–41.

Howell, John Thomas. 1942. New western plants. *Leaflets of Western Botany* 3 (6): 138–142.

Jepson, Willis Linn. 1914. *Lewisia.* In *A Flora of California.* Vol. 1. Berkeley: Associated Students Store, University of California.

Kruckeberg, Arthur. 1957. Documented chromosome numbers of plants. *Madroño* 14:111–112.

Lawrence, George H. M. 1951. *Taxonomy of Vascular Plants.* New York: Macmillan.

LePiniec, Marcel. 1964. Lewisias of the Siskiyous. *Bulletin of the American Rock Garden Society* 22 (1): 4–6.

Mathew, Brian. 1989. *The Genus Lewisia.* Bromley, Kent: Christopher Helm; Portland, Ore.: Timber Press, in association with the Royal Botanic Gardens, Kew.

de Mezey, Albert. 1972. Comments on new species, varieties, and the naming of plants. *Bulletin of the American Rock Garden Society* 30 (2): 41–44.

Millard, Frederick W. 1935. Lewisias at Camla. *Journal of the Royal Horticultural Society* 60: 159–161.

Munz, Philip A. 1959. Portulacaceae. In *A California Flora*. Berkeley: University of California Press. 2d ed., with supplement, 1969.

Nye, Clarice Paul. 1952. Treasures unawares. *Bulletin of the American Rock Garden Society* 10 (1): 50–52.

Palmer, Edward. 1871. Food products of the North American Indians. In *Report of the Commissioner of Agriculture for the Year 1870*. Washington, D.C.: Government Printing Office.

Parizek, Bedrich. 1986. Some experiences in breeding lewisias. *Bulletin of the American Rock Garden Society* 44 (3): 193–196.

Preece, W. H. N. 1937. *North American Rock Plants*. New York: Macmillan.

Pursh, Frederick T. 1814. *Lewisia*. In *Flora Americae Septentrionalis*. Vol. 1. London: White, Cochrane.

Robinson, Benjamin L. 1897. *Lewisia*. In *Synoptical Flora of North America*. Vol. 1. Ed. Asa Gray et al. New York.

Rydberg, Per Axel. 1906. Portulacaceae. In *Flora of Colorado*. Agricultural Experiment Station Bulletin 100, Fort Collins, Colo.

———. 1922. *Lewisia*. In *Flora of the Rocky Mountains and Adjacent Plains*. 2d ed. New York: privately printed.

———. 1932. Portulacaceae. In *North American Flora*. Vol. 21. New York: New York Botanical Garden.

Stebbins, G. Ledyard. 1968. *California Horticultural Society Newsletter* (December).

Taylor, L. E. 1951. *1951 Rock Plant Conference Report*. Vancouver, B.C.: Alpine Garden Club of British Columbia.

Torrey, John, and Asa Gray. 1840. Portulacaceae. In *A Flora of North America*. Vol. 1. New York: Wiley & Putnam.

Tucker, J. M., L. K. Mann, and S. L. Holloway. 1964. A natural hybrid in the genus *Lewisia*. *Cactus and Succulent Journal* 36:47–50.

Walkey, David. 1991. A century of alpines. In *Report of the Sixth International Rock Garden Plant Conference*. Warwick, U.K.: Alpine Garden Society.

Wallace, David Rains. 1983. *The Klamath Knot: Explorations of Myth and Evolution.* San Francisco: Sierra Club Books.

Watson, Sereno. 1871. Botany. In *Report of the U.S. Geological Exploration of the Fortieth Parallel* (U.S. Army, Engineering Dept., Professional Papers 18). Washington, D.C.: Government Printing Office.

———. 1875. Descriptions of new plants. *Proceedings of the American Academy of Arts and Sciences* 10.

Zwinger, Ann H., and Beatrice E. Willard. 1972. *The Land above the Trees: A Guide to American Alpine Tundra.* New York: Harper & Row.

Distribution Maps

Distribution of the six species comprising section *Cotyledon* SEAN HOGAN

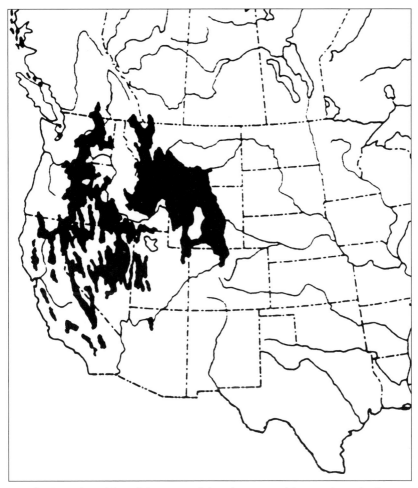

Distribution of *Lewisia rediviva* var. *rediviva,* the most widespread species in section *Lewisia* SEAN HOGAN

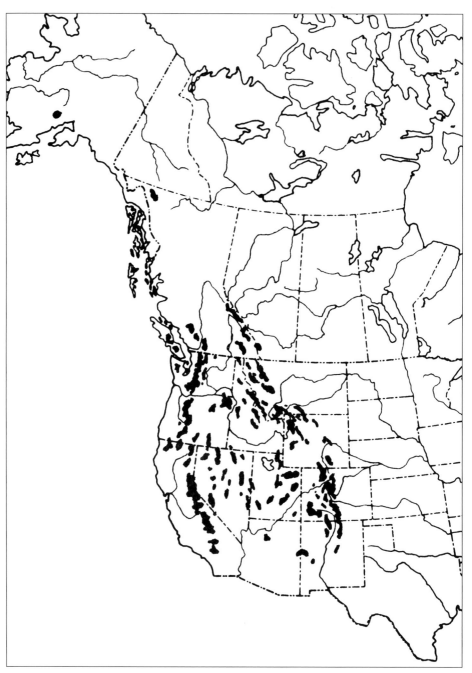

Distribution of *Lewisia pygmaea:* note that all species within section *Pygmaea* are encompassed within the boundaries of its range, and note too the recently reported disjunct populations near the Alaska-Yukon border and in the Alaska Range SEAN HOGAN

Distribution of *Lewisia tweedyi,* the sole member of subgenus *Strophiolum*
SEAN HOGAN

Index

Illustrations of or connected with the entry in question are indicated by **bold-faced** page numbers.

A Note from the Artist

The last several years have been the most wondrous adventure, as I have traveled with Roy and other friends through the alpine heights and river canyons of the West, seeking colonies of *Lewisia*. For Roy and me, another lewisia, "just ten miles off the road," always beckoned, and we left few stones unturned or mountains unclimbed in our quest.

My color plates are the composite of the countless photos, field observations, and sketches made on these trips. The execution of these illustrations was a monumental undertaking for me, and I hope that I have not taken too much artistic freedom in my attempt to emphasize the distinguishing characteristics of each species.

I owe my appreciation to all my friends and family, who patiently supported me as I worked on this project, and I dedicate my efforts to them as well as to the memory of two wonderful fellow artists, mentors, and friends, Jay Tronsdale and Kevin Nicolay, both of whom were taken from this world far too soon.

MICHEAL MOSHIER

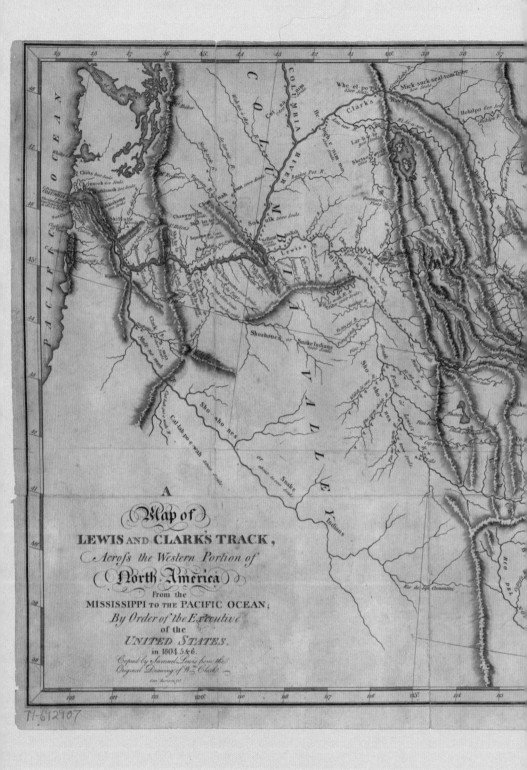

A
Map of
LEWIS AND CLARK'S TRACK,
Across the Western Portion of
North America
From the
MISSISSIPPI TO THE PACIFIC OCEAN;
By Order of the Executive
of the
UNITED STATES.
in 1804. 5 & 6.
Copied by Samuel Lewis from the
Original Drawing of W. Clark.